Policy Papers
in International Affairs

NUMBER 18

Contemporary Islamic Movements in Historical Perspective

Ira M. Lapidus

Institute of
International Studies

iiS

UNIVERSITY OF CALIFORNIA • BERKELEY

In sponsoring the Policy Papers in International Affairs series, the Institute of International Studies reasserts its commitment to a vigorous policy debate by providing a forum for innovative approaches to important policy issues. The views expressed in each paper are those of the author only, and publication in this series does not constitute endorsement by the Institute.

International Standard Book Number 0-87725-518-0

Library of Congress Card Number 83-82308

CONTENTS

Acknowledgments

This paper is based upon a larger work in progress on the role of Islam in the national development of Muslim societies and the history of Islamic societies from their origins to the present day. The research for the larger project has been generously supported by the Institute of International Studies of the University of Calfiornia, Berkeley. I would like to express my thanks to Professor Carl Rosberg, Director of the Institute, to Mrs. Karin Beros, Management Services Officer of the Institute, and to the Institute staff, who have been not only helpful but also gracious and generous in their support. The project has also been assisted by a year in residence at the Center for Advanced Studies in the Behavioral Sciences, Stanford, California, with the support of the National Endowment for the Humanities, and by a research grant from the Hoover Institution, Stanford University. To these institutions I express my deep appreciation for affording me the opportunity to concentrate upon research and writing.

In this survey and analysis of Muslim world developments, I have been assisted by both students and colleagues. I am grateful for the collaboration of Corinne Blake on Arab nationalism, Margaret Malamud on Iran, Dr. James Reid on the Ottoman and Safavid empires, and Drs. David Gilmartin and Sandria Freitag on the Indian subcontinent. They have helped me comprehend this subject by commenting on the scholarly literature and sharing with me their understanding. I am especially grateful to Drs. Elaine Combs-Schilling and Barbara Metcalf for the many conversations which have shaped and refined my views about Islamic societies. I would also like to thank Paul Gilchrist, Principal Editor of the Institute, for his thoughtful work on this paper and the many improvements he has suggested. I remain, of course, fully responsible for the views presented in this paper.

I. M. L.

I

INTRODUCTION

Like a desert wind which rises and subsides unexpectedly, the Islamic revival has come and gone from our consciousness. Though we recognize that it is an important phenomenon, we cannot say what it is and why it is significant. Our first response was concern that our strategic interests would be involved. The revolution in Iran raised exaggerated fears of a worldwide upheaval that could only benefit the Soviet Union and harm friendly regimes and American interests. In some circles the initial fears were followed by equally extravagant hopes that Islam could be used to subvert Soviet interests in Central Asia and elsewhere. For a moment the spectre of an unnamed third world force came into view. These fears and hopes were followed by more realistic assessments of Islamic and Middle Eastern situations. As newspaper coverage and analysis became more sophisticated, both political leaders and the general public came to understand the Islamic religion better, and to realize that the Middle East is linked to a much wider universe of Islamic countries. They became aware that there is more to the Middle East than the Arab-Israeli problem, and that the stability of the Persian Gulf region is central to American interests. At this juncture, however, despite the continuation of the revolution in Iran, the Soviet occupation of Afghanistan, the change of regime in Egypt, the war between Iran and Iraq, and the manifest weakness of all the Arab regimes, the Islamic revival has fallen from view. Only a handful of specialists can say what is happening in the Middle East and throughout the Islamic world.

Our difficulties in understanding Middle Eastern and Islamic world affairs are not surprising. The span of our attention for Middle East and Islamic matters has always been limited. We have always found it difficult to form a settled judgment about the area, to diagnose what is happening, and to design a policy which can be consistently applied. Some of these difficulties may be explained by the complexity of the regional situation. The Middle East is composed of numerous self-interested and vociferous states; it is a region of intense conflicts, of rapid and volatile changes in political regimes, economic conditions, and international relations. The very fact that the region has numerous small states helps project its quarrels onto the international scene, as opposed to the great continental-scale nation-states such as India, Indonesia, or China, which absorb them within.

Some of our difficulties, however, can only be explained by our own passions and prejudices, our own mental sets and motivations. The Islamic world throws us into confusion because of the centrality of religious issues. Most of us have strong feelings about religion. Humanists and secularists, convinced that the modern world is turning from religious values and allegiances to secular societies, who see religion as an irrational and backward form of human consciousness, are confounded by the continuing importance of religious belief and affiliations among Middle Eastern Muslims, Christians, and Jews. No events have confused interpreters of modernization and change more thoroughly than the revolution in Iran, which despite all denials, past and present, turns out to be a revolution led by religious teachers in the name of Islam and supported by people inspired by religious conviction. Equally shocking to the view that the world is evolving from outmoded religious ways of thinking toward secular humanistic and nationalist forms of society is the tenacity of Israeli and Zionist dreams and the passionate Jewish and Muslim, not to speak of Christian, feelings about Jerusalem.*

People who have religious convictions or are sympathetic to the argument that religion matters in political affairs are not necessarily

---

*Christians also have a direct emotional involvement in the problems of Israel and Jerusalem. American and western support for Israel is based on many considerations, one of which is Christian eschatology. At the time of the Balfour Declaration, British cabinet opinion was influenced by messianic feelings about the significance of the return of Israel to Zion. Similar feelings help explain the support for Israel among American Christian fundamentalist denominations.

more clear-sighted. Christians and Jews often do not take Islam seriously. They are convinced that Islam is an inferior religion, a latecomer, a poor copy of older faiths, established by fraud or by force, or winning converts by appeals to self-interest. They cannot believe that Muslims are genuinely committed to their religion as the highest expression of God's revelation and the closest approximation to the truth. Reciprocally, Muslims often do not understand why Jews and Christians should remain attached to outmoded religions when a more definitive version has been revealed. While Jews and Christians think Islam must be fake because it is new, Muslims think that Judaism and Christianity must be corrupt because they are old. In addition, anti-Semitism is a potent source of opinion about Middle Eastern affairs.

Furthermore, many Europeans, Americans, and Middle Easterners, Jews, Christians, and Muslims, are aware of a long history of antagonism and warfare between Christian and Muslim peoples. This hostility began with the Islamic invasions of the Middle East and North Africa, continued through the Crusades, the Turkish conquest of the Balkans and Central Europe, the Balkan wars of the nineteenth century, the bitter problems of the Greeks and the Armenians, and twentieth-century European imperialism. The legacy of Mediterranean, European, and Middle Eastern confrontation has for Europeans and Americans largely been smoothed over by the last century of European domination and by forgetfulness of history, but it is very much alive in the lately colonized Middle Eastern and Muslim world. In both religion and politics, Islam still appears to westerners as a closely related but rival civilization.

There is yet another reason for our perplexity, confusion, and incomprehension of the Middle East and Islamic world—that is its "otherness." Edward Said is only the latest writer to point out that Middle Eastern peoples, indeed all Eastern peoples, serve us as a psychological other.* They are the outsider, the repository of our negative self-image, the object of our fantasy projections. "We" are rational, self-controlled, mature, hard-working, productive, and creative; "they" are irresponsible, emotional, sensual, self-indulgent, and

*Edward Said, *Orientalism* (New York: Pantheon, 1978).

disorderly. We attribute to them the same qualities whites attribute to blacks, or men to women. Therefore they are not "real" people with whom we can deal on a basis of mutual comprehension and respect. Muslims in return have their own way of mythicizing westerners. To Iranians, Americans and Britishers are manipulative devils who control all events, playing havoc with Iranian interests and threatening to subvert decency and order in Iranian society. In their minds, Christians are the source of the immorality of women, the corruption of governments, and the exploitation of the poor by the rich.

These barriers to comprehension may not be unique to the Middle East, and may typify our way of apprehending the world in general, but in Middle Eastern and Islamic affairs such attitudes are less well corrected by reliable information and by informed rational discussion. The need for serious consideration of the actualities of cultural, religious, and political situations in the Middle East and in other Islamic regions is acute.

This paper is intended to provide a basic introduction to Islam and Islamic movements, and to the political and religious actualities of the contemporary Middle East and other Muslim world areas, in an historical perspective. The Islamic revival is a complex phenomenon, and here it will be considered from two points of view: (a) in terms of international, Muslim worldwide religious and political action and (b) in terms of individual movements within a national political context. The first point of view will give us some insights into the cultural and political concepts common to all of them; the second will enable us to understand why Islamic revival movements are so different and have such different consequences in different countries. Primary emphasis will be on the religious and political aspects of these movements; issues of economic development and technological change, though highly relevant, will be less fully considered. In this case the political and cultural factors that define Islamic movements better enable us to account for the variations among them, as well as their differences from ideological and political movements in other societies. The basic premise underlying this paper is that an understanding of current developments in the Muslim world requires an understanding of deeply rooted patterns of Islamic values and Islamic social and political institutions, and how they operate in a modern and changing political and economic environment. An historical analysis helps to identify the basic structural factors and long-term trends in Muslim societies, and to distinguish them from accidental elements and short-term tendencies.

II

THE HISTORICAL BACKGROUND OF THE CONTEMPORARY ISLAMIC REVIVAL

Though Islamic revival movements have for the moment receded from our consciousness, they continue unabated. They are a deep-rooted historical phenomenon and probably an abiding feature of Islamic societies. The Islamic revival which caught our attention in the 1970s was only the latest in a series of Islamic political and reform movements going back to the eighteenth century. To understand these movements we have to begin by discussing the basic structure of Muslim societies before the modern era, and comprehend how Muslims themselves have articulated the ongoing political, economic, and cultural struggles in their own societies. This is not history for the sake of history because these basic structures continue to be important for understanding what is happening in the modern world.

Islam had its origins in the preaching of the prophet Muhammad in Mecca and Medina in the early seventh century A.D. From the seventh to the eighteenth century, Islam spread by conquest, trade, missionary-preaching, and migration from its Arabian homeland throughout much of the Old World. Islamic populations were established in the Middle East, the Balkans, Africa, Central Asia, India, and Southeast Asia as far as the Philippines. Great Islamic empires, including the Ottoman (c. 1280-1923), the Safavid (1500-1722) and Qajar (1779-1925), and the Mughal (1526-1857), governed large regions of the Middle East and South Asia. Lesser Muslim regimes controlled parts of Indonesia, Malaysia, and North and West Africa.

In many of these Islamic societies a pattern of social and political institutions came into being that helps define the political role of Islam. For the purposes of discussion we may say that Islamic societies historically have been composed at base of small-scale, local communities organized and identified in lineage, tribal, and ethnic terms. Every Islamic society has been built upon a population of diverse peoples who have preserved their own kinship systems, territorial divisions, linguistic and ethnic groupings, and other non-Islamic cultural features.

In these societies, Islam was articulated at two levels—as a culture of beliefs and practices rooted in the consciousness of individuals, and in the form of religious communities. Islam was not a single religion but a "family" of religious beliefs and religious movements. All Muslims identified with a particular community and version of Islam, and considered themselves either Sunnis, Shi'a, or Kharijis. The distinctions go back to early seventh-century political disputes over succession to the leadership of the Muslim community which hardened into differences of ritual and legal practices and theological beliefs. The Sunnis are those Muslims—now the majority—who accept the actual historic succession of the early caliphs and the particular legal codes, theological doctrines, and mystic exercises evolved within that group. The Shi'a are those Muslims who believe that only the fourth caliph, Ali, was the rightful successor of the prophet and that only his descendants should have succeeded him. They are a substantial minority concentrated mainly in Iran, Pakistan and India, and East Africa. Since the ninth century they have split into numerous subsects divided over the question of the proper line of descent in the family of Ali. The Kharijis, now a very tiny minority in Africa, are those sectarians who oppose dynastic succession and favor election to the caliphate. Each of the major bodies is itself divided into schools, brotherhoods, and sects, as well as followers and devotees of particular teachers and holy men and worshippers at particular shrines.

In any given territory there were ordinarily several levels of Muslim associations. From a Muslim state, Muslims expected support for religion, protection against infidel enemies, and patronage for scholars and holy men. The ruler was a symbol of the existence of the legitimate Muslim political order, the guarantor of the principle

7

that Muslim laws would be enforced, and the symbol of the historic continuity of Muslim communities. Muslims regarded their states and empires as the ultimate protectors of the holy law and the holy society. Muslim commoners were only subjects and not citizens, but they nonetheless had a stake in the political regimes as an expression of their Muslim identity.

At the same time the Sunni Muslim populations of any given territory or regime considered themselves members of a school of religious law. A school of law was an association adhering to the codes of law developed by discussion and debate among legal scholars in the eighth and ninth centuries, and then codified, somewhat in the fashion of the more familiar Talmud, into presentations of legal principles or rules, and discussions of their precedents and implications. These legal teachings were the preserve of specialist scholars called *ulama*, who were primarily students and teachers of the law, but also were notaries, legal advisers, and judges. The scholars organized Muslim education, judicial administration, and charitable activities. A penumbra of students, patrons, and adherents, including government officials, merchants, and artisans, made a school of law a socio-communal body. The schools were usually supported by state regimes and sometimes organized into a bureaucratic administration under state control. Four such schools were founded in Sunni Muslim countries. In most Middle Eastern countries the Hanafi school was favored by the state authorities, but the Shafi'i, Maliki, and Hanbali schools also received government patronage and had a popular following. In Iran the Shi'a ulama formed an analogous body.

Muslims were also participants in Sufi brotherhoods. Sufism is Muslim mysticism, or the spiritual discipline which leads to direct experience of the reality of God's being. The term is extremely elastic, however, and refers to a great variety of religious beliefs and practices. This is not the place to discuss the varieties of Sufism except to say that the term covers two basic constellations of religious ideas. One kind of Sufism is a religious and ethical discipline built upon adherence to the teachings of the Qur'an, the *hadith* (the sayings of the prophet), and the law, supplemented by spiritual practices designed to cultivate an outward conformity to Muslim norms and an inner insight into the ultimate spiritual realities. Sufism from this point of view is commonly integrated with the ulama schools of law, and the ordinary Sufi of this type is at once a scholar and a spiritual master. For convenience we can refer to this type of Sufism as law-Sufism.

Muslim holy men of this type, who cultivate religious knowledge, ethical discipline, and spiritual insight, become the leaders of religious and even political associations. The basic Sufi-led community is composed of the individual holy man and his disciples and occasional devotees. A Sufi holy man can also be the founder of a lineage. When the holy man and his disciples reckon themselves to be the descendants of earlier teachers and the brothers of other groups who have a similar genealogy, they form a religious brotherhood or *tariqa*. Sufis also help organize corporate bodies such as guilds and confederations among kinship groups and tribal peoples by providing them with shared religious beliefs and ceremonies. A Sufi brotherhood can also give political unity to diverse ethnic, lineage, or tribal groups by bringing them into a larger, religiously defined affiliation.

A second kind of Sufism is belief in Sufi saints. To many ordinary believers, a Sufi is a person who has attained a quality of inner consciousness which makes him close to God, and therefore a person to be venerated as an intermediary between the spiritual and the material worlds. The Sufi is a miracle worker and a dispenser of blessings to those who believe in him. While the first type of Sufism leads to the internalization of ritual and moral discipline, the second type leads to the veneration of the person of the holy man, his tomb or shrine, and his descendants and disciples as the heirs of his *baraka* (spiritual power), and to a religious life of offering sacrifices and communal festivals around the shrines of the saints. This shrine-Sufism is a religion of magical acquisition of divine powers rather than a religion of ethical or emotional self-cultivation. Though both types are called Islam, and both are Sufism, they represent profoundly contrasting concepts of the religious life.

This second type of Sufism also has a communal or political expression. Commonly the tomb of the original saint becomes an institution, administered by his descendants, who maintain the tomb and regulate the ceremonies associated with it. Shrines of this type are endowed with agricultural estates to provide funds for their upkeep and for charitable activities. The tomb complex becomes the focus of a community composed of all the people who believe that the saint can perform miracles and who worship at the tomb. In such a case, however, the community or fellowship of believers remains highly diffuse, segmented, and little capable of organized group activity.

The two main types of Sufism embody a great variety of religious and social practices. Sufism of either the law or the shrine type refers both to the spiritual practices of individuals and to the brotherhoods formed by devotees of these practices. In the Islamic religion the individual Sufi adept may subscribe to a wide variety of religious or theosophical beliefs and practices, may come from any walk of life, may have multiple affiliations (including simultaneous membership in different schools of law and Sufi brotherhoods), and may couple his mystical insights and practices with any of a number of worldly vocations, combining the roles of Sufi and scholar, merchant, artisan, or political chieftain. Similarly, the disciples and followers, while united by their adherence to the master and to the religious practices of their order, represent every conceivable social milieu. Given all this variation, Sufism cannot be generally defined, but can only be described in each particular case. The underlying common factor is the exercise of religious insight, discipline, or authority in worldly affairs and a reputation for sanctity.

By the eighteenth century, these several forms of state, ulama, and Sufi Islam, and the numerous communal groups of each type, made up the fabric of Islamic societies. The several forms of Islamic belief and community represented different political and social milieus, different economic interest groups, and different religious values. In each Muslim region there were numerous brotherhood and shrine communities, often in religious or political competition with each other. In the eighteenth century, this competition became more intense. The weakening of major Muslim empires, including the Ottoman, the Safavid, and the Mughal, and the attendant and consequent expansion of European colonial powers in the eighteenth and nineteenth centuries broke down the established balance of political and religious forces in Muslim societies. In the course of the late eighteenth, nineteenth, and early twentieth centuries, the Dutch seized control of Java, the British established their paramountcy in India, and the French colonized North and West Africa. Russia occupied much of Central Asia between 1864 and 1885. By World War I most of Africa was under colonial control. The nominally independent Ottoman and Qajar Muslim empires in Turkey, the Arab world, and Iran fell under British and Russian tutelage. By subduing and destroying indigenous Muslim states, European intervention opened the way to intensified internal struggle in Muslim countries over issues of authority, distribution of power, and cultural and political goals. This struggle lasts to the present day. In modern times two main competing tendencies have appeared. One is Muslim reformism or revivalism, and the other is Muslim modernism and secularism. The former is the immediate background for the present Islamic revival, but the two must be understood in conjunction to grasp the problems of political and religious identity in the contemporary Muslim world.

The first Muslim response to the breakup of the worldwide system of Muslim empires was the growth of reformist, revivalist, or "scripturalist" movements. These movements began in the seventeenth and eighteenth centuries among scattered Muslim ulama and law-minded Sufis in the Ottoman empire, India, and North Africa. In Cairo and Arabia informal study groups representing Muslims from India, Iraq, Morocco, and other places espoused a purified version of Islamic belief and practice based on the study of the Qur'an, hadith, and law, combined with a Sufi mysticism which stressed meditation and asceticism as the basis of Muslim spirituality. The imitation of the prophet Muhammad became their ideal of a Muslim life. These reformers, aided by the conviction that God was punishing Muslims for failure to heed His will, opposed the tolerant attitude of Muslim state regimes toward non-Muslim peoples and cultures, and sought to abolish saint worship and the more florid religious cults and ceremonies and to dispel superstitious or magical beliefs and practices. In their view, worship of saints was not Muslim at all, but polytheistic and pagan. Their goal was to integrate ordinary people into reformed Sufi brotherhoods. They were committed, if need be, to militant action to destroy corrupt versions of Islam and to create a just and truly Islamic community. This was the origin of the first modern Islamic revival; it arose out of internal debates among Muslims over religious beliefs and values and as an internal reaction to the spread of cultic Sufi forms of Islam. It was a movement of reform within the "church." Foreign intervention, however, would both consolidate the reformist trends in Muslim religious affairs and turn reformist movements into anticolonial resistance.

The reform tendency had its first major success in Arabia in the mid-eighteenth century, where the Wahhabi movement, born out of an alliance of a reform preacher with the Saudi family, united diverse tribal groups into a movement which conquered most of Arabia. From Mecca, Medina, and Arabia the influence of reform teachings spread to other parts of the Muslim world. India and southeast Asia, which were in continuous interaction with the holy cities, due to the travels of merchants, scholars, and pilgrims, soon came under reformist influence. The reform movement burst into political agitation in Bengal and the Northwest Frontier Provinces in the 1820s and 1830s, and was partly directed against Sikh and British rulers. One of the important early reformers, Sayyid Ahmad Barēlwi (1786-1831), organized Pathan resistance to the British in the Northwest Frontier Provinces, and though defeated and killed in 1831, propagated Muslim reformist activity which led to the founding of Deoband, the great reformist seminary, and to a series of missionary programs lasting to the present. The reform movement had similarly profound effects in Indonesia. Pilgrims and scholars returning to Sumatra in the early nineteenth century launched the Padri movement in an attempt to Islamize Muslim villagers in Minangkabau. Later, reform activists helped support the Acheh resistance to Dutch expansion in northern Sumatra.

In Central Asia the Naqshbandi Sufi order became the bearer of new religious inspiration and ultimately of political resistance to Russian and Chinese expansion. Naqshbandi activists in the Caucasus, the Volga, and Khazan regions organized local resistance to Russian domination. In Turkistan the shaykhs of Khokand fought the imposition of Chinese rule. As far off as Yunan, Muslim activists inspired "new sect" rebellions between 1856 and 1873.

In West Africa, Islamic reform had both indigenous roots and international Muslim connections. Eighteenth- and nineteenth-century reformist movements in the Senegambian region of West Africa were not connected with international movements, but represented a local tradition of Muslim resistance to political elites. Of similarly independent inspiration were the Fulani conquests led by Usman Don Fodio (1754-1817), which established the caliphate of Sokoto (1809-1904) in the region between the Niger and Lake Chad. International reformist influences were introduced by the Tijani order, which spread in Algeria, Morocco, and West Africa, and interacting with local forces eventually inspired the formation of the regime of al-Hajj Umar (1794?-1864) in the regions from the Niger to Senegal. Elsewhere the Sammani order spread through the Nilotic Sudan, Eritrea, and Ethiopia in the late nineteenth century, while the Idrisi won an important following in the Sudan. The Sanusi helped to unify tribal peoples in Libya and created a loosely organized state which resisted Italian conquest.

Thus, throughout the Muslim world reformist movements began with a program of internal religious and communal revitalization and then became the spearhead of anticolonial resistance. In the late nineteenth and early twentieth centuries, European colonial administrators and European public opinion were intensely aware of Islamic activism and saw it as a worldwide conspiracy to throw off western domination. They saw Islam entirely in its national and political guise, and did not comprehend the internal and religious bases of Islamic strength. Nor did they comprehend how fragmented Islamic reform movements were, and how little capable of unified political action.

The late nineteenth-century confrontation of European and Muslim peoples not only channelled the reform movement into anticolonial resistance, but also generated a second major trend of Muslim thought and political action. This trend is best characterized as Muslim modernism. The essential principle of modernism is that the political defeat of Muslims at the hands of European powers had revealed the military and political vulnerability of Muslim states and peoples in contrast to the strength and vitality of European

13

civilization. In the view of the modernists, the restoration of the political power of Muslim societies required them to adapt themselves to the modern world. This meant borrowing European military techniques, centralizing state power, modernizing economies, and providing a modern education for the military and political elites. It also meant that the medieval forms of Islamic civilization had to be repudiated and Islam reconstructed on the basis of the principles of rationality, ethical activism, and nationalism. Reform of the state had to be based on a total modernization of Muslim societies. Only this kind of revitalization, they argued, would enable Muslims to maintain their position in the modern world.

Muslim modernism was the doctrine not of ulama or Sufis but of sections of the political elite and a new western-educated intelligentsia. The modernist point of view was first espoused by the Young Ottoman intelligentsia in the 1860s and 1870s. They called upon the endangered Ottoman regime to transform itself into a constitutional government, and to promote a social morality and a revived cultural life based on a simplified Turkish language. The Young Ottomans remained committed nonetheless to the principles of Islam. Similarly, in India, Sayyid Ahmad Khan (1817-1898) argued that the survival of Indian Muslims under British rule required the education of a new generation of Muslim leaders loyal to the principles of Islam but adapted to the political and scientific culture of the modern world. While the Ottoman and Indian intelligentsia were concerned with local situations, Jamal al-din al-Afghani (1839-1897), an Iranian Muslim agitator, traveled and proselytized everywhere for an international union of Muslim peoples committed to the modernization of Islam and to political unity in the face of colonial oppression. Islamic modernism, then, was essentially the expression of political or former political elites who were concerned with the restoration of state power but who understood the broad social and cultural bases of power.

Muslim modernism could be blended with Islamic reformism. Under the influence of al-Afghani, a young Egyptian religious scholar, Muhammad Abduh (1849-1905), combined the reformist principles—return to Qur'an and the sayings of the prophet, the right of independent judgment in religious matters, abandonment of a stifling conformity to outmoded tradition, and opposition to cultic Sufi practices—with a modernist responsiveness to the political and cultural pressures of Europe. Abduh, like his mentor, believed both in Muslim patriotism and unity in the struggle for autonomy from Europe and in adapting Islam to the needs of the modern world. This blend of modernist and reformist thought inspired the Salafiya movement, which spread through Egypt, the Arab world, and North Africa, and the Muhammadiya movement in Indonesia. Both these movements, whose influence continues to the present day, are scripturalist in orientation, devoted to the reform of education as a correction to shrine and saint worship and magical religious practices, and committed to the need for adjustment to modern economic and technological conditions. Both movements are latently political in that they cultivate a consciousness of the need for autonomy from European power if the vitality of Islamic states and societies is to be restored.

Though the reformist and the modernist movements could be blended, they represented two quite different Muslim responses to the problems of internal political decline and foreign occupation of Muslim countries. The modernist movements arose among political elites and westernized intelligentsia, and were primarily concerned with a restoration of Muslim state power. The reformist movements arose essentially in religious circles, and were primarily concerned with problems of Muslim religious consciousness and communal organization, though they were often mobilized for anticolonial political purposes. By the early twentieth century the modernist and the reformist movements, in their several guises, were the most vital internal forces in Muslim societies.

The contemporary phase of the Islamic revival derives from this historical background but is profoundly transformed. While the nineteenth-century Islamic reform movements were reactions to the breakdown of Muslim empires and to European domination, the present revival is a reaction to the formation of modern national and secular states throughout the Muslim world. Some of these, like Turkey and Iran, were founded after World War I, but most, such as the Arab states and Pakistan, have become independent since World War

II. In the Persian Gulf region new states were formed as recently as the 1960s. Most of these states are governed by the ideological heirs to the nineteenth-century political elites and intelligentsia, and pursue secular and nationalist policies of economic, social, and cultural development which lead to the further breakdown of traditional communities and values. At the same time new generations of religious reformers hark back to the basic religious and political principles of the revivalist movements. At stake is the allegiance of millions of people who belong neither to the modernist nor to the reformist camp, but are still committed to traditional societies and traditional forms of Islamic belief and association.

The present revival is a multifaceted response to the new political structure and economic conditions of Muslim societies. It takes the form of a worldwide enhanced interest in and practice of Islam as more people go to prayer, pilgrimage, and read and write books about Islam. International Muslim contacts at conferences, pilgrimages to Mecca and Medina, Sufi meetings, and the mass media have everywhere stimulated Muslim consciousness of the importance of religious as opposed to national identity.

Furthermore, in many Muslim countries there is a renewal of religious and political reform movements aimed at making active Muslims out of nominal believers. Missionary and reformist associations are active in Turkey, Egypt, Iran, Pakistan, Malaysia, and other Muslim countries. Some of them have their origins in nineteenth-century Islamic Sufi reform movements, and have primarily religious goals such as the purification of religious practice and the elimination of saint worship, magical beliefs, and popular festivals in order to concentrate the attention of believers upon prayer, formal obedience to the teachings of Muslim law, and intellectual pursuits. Some of these reformist movements, such as the Muslim Brotherhood in Egypt and the Muhammadiya in Indonesia, have a modernizing orientation, and see the correct and true practice of Islam as consistent with the demands of modern society for a disciplined life, active engagement in economic and political affairs, a strong sense of communal responsibility, and patriotic commitment to national interests. They sponsor schools, orphanages, scout groups, cottage industries, women's auxiliaries, and political parties. Some of them go so far as to espouse Islam as a comprehensive blueprint for a modern way of life, and call for the formation of Islamic states to enforce Islamic morality. The Muslim Brotherhood in Egypt, the Jama'at-i Islami in Pakistan, and the Muhammadiya in Indonesia have at times attempted to control national states.

The political implications of this latest revival of Muslim self-consciousness and reformist activity vary with the national context. In some Muslim countries, established, conservative, even secularized regimes are backtracking to give at least lip service, and sometimes moral and financial support, to Islamic religious principles and religious groups. Algeria, Libya, the Gulf states, Pakistan, and Iran identify themselves as Muslim states or as states serving the Muslim cause in order to win legitimacy and acceptance from otherwise restless populations. Oil-rich Muslim countries, especially Saudi Arabia and the Gulf states, actively promote Islamic preaching, missionary reform, and political movements. Under Saudi auspices new pan-Islamic organizations, such as the World Muslim League founded in 1962 and the Islamic Conference of Foreign Ministers organized in 1969, support Muslim cultural centers, news and broadcasting agencies, Islamic banks, and political activities.

In many other states, Islam is becoming the rallying cry of interest groups opposed to prevailing regimes. In Nigeria, peasants forced to leave the countryside and seek work in Kano organize Islamic community groups under the leadership of rural religious teachers to press their economic interests as laborers. In Malaysia, small-scale peasant landowners have organized under the banner of Islam to resist the pressures that deprive them of ownership of land. In Egypt, students and professionals take up Islam as a means of adjusting traditional, moral, and social values to the realities of the new economic and political situation. And, finally, Islam served in the Iranian revolution to generate a coalition of displaced peasants, petit bourgeois artisans and merchants, students, and other groups to overthrow the regime of the late shah. In all of these societies a deep resistance has built up among the dislocated parts of the population who have sacrificed cultural integrity and economic well-being for the sake of state

17

military or political policies or state-led efforts at economic development which in the end have not benefitted them. Widespread frustration and resentment of the sacrifices made in the name of modernity have inspired a reaction and a demand for a return to the proven bases of cultural tradition.

Thus, looked at overall, the Islamic revival has varied and even contradictory religious and political implications. It appears sometimes as a movement of religious worship or of social reform, sometimes as the banner of political opposition in the interest of particular groups or classes, and sometimes as a form of legitimation for dominant regimes. It sometimes appears to be in favor of and sometimes against state power and economic modernization. In fact, Islamic concepts and rhetoric seem almost universally adaptable as a language of both social protest and political legitimation. To better understand the reasons for this burst of Islamic activity, we shall look at several major cases in detail in order to determine the special character of the various movements, their differing symbols and goals, and their distinctive roles in the different political and economic settings in which they have developed. On the basis of these case studies, we can attempt to explain the apparent contradictions the Islamic revival presents when viewed in global perspective.

III

CASE STUDIES: ISLAM IN NATIONAL CONTEXTS

The contemporary Muslim revival is an international movement which has its origins in Muslim reaction to the formation of secular national states. However, in each country the conditions for the formation of modern states and for the organization of a Muslim opposition are unique. To be understood properly, the revival has to be examined in each national context. In this chapter, we shall review developments in four states and one group of states. We shall consider the states which descend from the former Ottoman empire: (1) Turkey, (2) Egypt, and (3) the Arab fertile crescent countries, including Syria, Iraq, and Jordan (leaving aside Lebanon, Israel, and the West Bank because of the many special complications in these areas); then (4) Iran, and (5) Pakistan.

1. TURKEY

Turkey came into being in 1923 as a phoenix rising from the ashes of the Ottoman empire. At the end of World War I, the Ottoman empire was defeated by the European allies, occupied, and partitioned into British, French, and Greek spheres of influence. Under the leadership of Mustafa Kemal, however, the remnants of the late Ottoman military elite organized a Turkish resistance, expelled the foreign occupying forces, defeated the Greeks, and brought a new Turkish republic into being. Turkey inherited the Ottoman tradition of centralized government and competent military leadership, a long history of nineteenth-century reform and modernization, and an intelligentsia of army officers, experienced administrators, engineers, technical

19

experts, and intellectuals. Modern Turkey thus came into being with a coherent state structure and a strong commitment to a state-directed society based on principles of nationalism, industrialization, and cultural secularization.

The primary goals of Kemalist Turkey were economic development and cultural reform. With Soviet loans and expertise, textile factories were built in the 1920s. In 1933, Turkey adopted its first five-year plan. The Sumer Bank was founded to finance textile, paper, glass, and sugar enterprises. Great Britain helped finance the construction of iron and steel works. In this period the foundations were set for the emergence of a modern industrial economy.

At the same time the Kemalist regime launched a cultural revolution. Mustafa Kemal and the Turkish elite sought to absorb the masses of the people into the ideological and cultural framework of the republican regime. They attempted to break the attachment of ordinary people to Islam and to win them to a western and secular style of life. The new regime abolished the organized institutions of Islam—the sultanate in 1923, the caliphate in 1924. The ministries for religious law were abolished. Religious endowments and ulama were put under the control of a new office of religious affairs. In 1925 the Sufi orders were declared illegal and disbanded. In principle, religion was disestablished and deprived of any role in public life. Remaining religious activities, such as worship, were brought under state control.

The republican regime also attacked the symbolic ties of Turkish Muslims with the past. In 1927 the wearing of the fez was forbidden. In 1928 a new Latin script was introduced to replace Arabic script, and an effort was begun to purify the Turkish language of its Arabic and Persian content. In 1935 all Turks were required to take surnames in the western fashion. A new family law based upon Swiss legal codes replaced the Muslim law. Not only was Islam disestablished but the ordinary symbols of Turkish attachment to traditional culture were replaced by new legal, linguistic, and other signs of modern identity.

Radical as were these economic and cultural policies, the Kemalist regime was not revolutionary. The cultural upheaval was not accompanied by social change. The dominant elites and organizations retained their authority, and no effort was made to mobilize the peasantry to participate in the new regime. The cultural changes imposed from the top had relatively slight penetration: they divided the country into a modernized urban elite and rural peasant masses oriented toward Islam. The combination of a radical cultural policy with conservative, statist political and social policies made Turkey one of the first examples of a new type of Asian nation—an authoritarian regime attempting to carry out radical economic and cultural reforms.

Mustafa Kemal died in 1938, but the regime continued under his loyal colleague, Ismet Inonu, until 1949. During the period between Kemal's death and the end of the Inonu regime, however, the way was prepared for a new political system. Economic development generated new groups of businessmen, factory managers, rural landowners, prosperous peasants, and intellectuals who wanted increased recognition and political participation. By the 1940s these new groups were no longer willing to accept the division of Turkish society into a governing urban elite and excluded provincial subjects. Also, post-World War II Turkish legislation relaxed government controls over commerce and the universities and increased the expectation of political participation. After World War II, the United States, which had become a powerful military and political patron of Turkey in opposition to the threat of Soviet expansion, began to exert pressure for a less paternalistic and more democratic system.

In 1946 the Inonu government allowed the formation of an opposition party—the Democrat party. In 1949 this party took power, representing rural and provincial interests and a coalition of peasants, landowners, and businessmen who wanted a more liberal regime and less strict control of the economy by the central government. Its rural supporters also wanted a liberalization of cultural policy and a partial restoration of Islam.

The Islamic loyalties of ordinary people had never been seriously disturbed. The Turkish populace continued to identify itself as Muslim, and throughout the republican era continued to carry on worship in mosques and at the tombs of saints in the traditional way. In 1949 the ruling Democrat party allowed the teaching of Islam in schools and reintroduced state support for mosques and Islamic worship. The government elites, however, remained on guard against a resurgence of Islamic organizations or any effort to reestablish Islamic policies in public affairs. The Sufi orders were held in check, and religious endowments were not restored. Nonetheless the Democrat party compromised Kemalist dogma by coupling economic modernization and Islamic restoration.

In the 1960s and 1970s Turkey entered an era of multiparty conflict. Further social and economic differentiation of the population brought increased political awareness and activism. Engineers and industrial workers—and militant ideological groups of both right and left—entered the political arena. The parliamentary system failed to contain these conflicts, and in 1960, 1971, and 1980 the army intervened to restore political order. In effect, economic and cultural change has made Turkey a highly pluralistic society which lacks effective political means to give coherent economic and ideological direction to the development of the country. In these conditions movements and parties committed to the re-Islamization of state and society grew stronger. The most important of these—the Sa'id Nursi movement, founded by a religious preacher and writer—achieved a wide underground following in Turkey despite the opposition of the government and the prosecution of Sa'id Nursi for religious agitation. His *Risala-i Nur*, widely read by small groups throughout the country, has cultivated a revived devotion to Islam. Naqshbandi and Tijani Sufi groups are also active. In the 1970s the National Salvation party, which favors the reestablishment of an Islamic state in Turkey, and is supported by engineers committed to technological progress and by small town and petit-bourgeois voters, won a small percentage of the vote in Turkish elections.

These movements represent both a revival of religious attachment and of Muslim political assertion. Striking in contemporary Turkey, however, is the relative weakness of the traditional forms of Islamic religious organization. The ulama and the traditional Sufi brotherhoods are of secondary importance. The two generations in which traditional ulama and Sufi forms of Islam were suppressed have channelled latent Islamic sentiment into new forms of Islamic organization.

While the revival of Islamic activism is of great contemporary importance, it remains so far a minority interest within contemporary Turkey. The complex social and political development of the country and the creation of a differentiated social structure have led to cross-currents of political and ideological interests which have submerged the traditional polarization between a secular state and Islamic religious values. To the traditional question of the role of Islam in the political society have been added questions of central and provincial interests, management versus worker interests, and army and bureaucratic administration as opposed to private entrepreneurship. In Turkey the Islamic revival is only one of several ideological developments, including socialist, capitalist, communist, Maoist, and other movements, fighting for power in a very pluralistic and changing society.

2. EGYPT

In Egypt, as in Turkey, the Islamic revival is a reaction to the formation of a secular national state, but it has a very different political role. Egypt was formally a province of the Ottoman empire, but was seized by Britain in 1882 and governed as a protectorate from 1914 to 1922. In 1922 a native Egyptian political elite of landowners, officials, journalists, and lawyers won partial independence and established a constitutional monarchy based on liberal principles. The liberal regime, however, failed to win full independence from Britain, failed to cope with the grave problems of economic inequality, and failed to give coherent ideological identity to the semi-independent nation. It failed because the Egyptian elites lacked direct continuity with the Ottoman heritage and the military capabilities, self-confidence, and authority of the Turks, and because they gradually lost confidence in Western constitutional and liberal values. Even in upper class and intellectual circles, there was a turn toward Islam in the 1930s.

The first Islamic revival in Egypt came in the 1930s and 1940s. It owed little to the traditional ulama or Sufi brotherhoods. Rather,

23

a new generation of Islamic preachers and teachers appealed to the old *effendi* class—people with a traditional Muslim education, such as clerks, minor civil servants, shopkeepers, students and others, who had been hurt by foreign occupation and by the change from Muslim to western education, and had been uprooted from their position in the old order of society. Islam also appealed to a new generation of students and industrial workers who were dissatisfied with the dominance of a landowning political elite committed to a foreign ideology.

The most important of the neo-Muslim movements was the Ikhwan al-Muslimin, or the Muslim Brotherhood. This was founded by Hasan al-Banna, a schoolteacher in Ismailiya, in 1928. To workers, the poor, students, and others, Hasan al-Banna preached the restoration of Islamic principles, return to the Qur'an, and resumption of Islamic piety. His preaching built up a movement with an extensive following. It was divided into cells or chapters and provided mosques, schools, clinics, and even cooperative work opportunities for its members. The Brotherhood became politically active in the mid-1930s, adding athletic and paramilitary groups. Volunteers were sent to support the Arab uprising in Palestine between 1936 and 1939. After World War II the Muslim Brotherhood became the most powerful political movement in Egypt. It condemned the corruption of the Egyptian regime and its failures in the Palestine-Israel war of 1948-1949, and supplied guerrilla fighters to oppose continued British occupation of the Suez Canal zone in 1950-1951. It also sponsored violent demonstrations and strikes against the government.

The Muslim Brotherhood represented not only a political but also an ideological alternative to the liberal regime. It proposed the establishment of an Islamic government—a representative government based on consultation with the ulama and devoted to the application of Muslim law in public life. It proposed a regulated economy in accord with a combination of Islamic and socialist principles. Specifically, the Brotherhood stood for nationalization of utilities and a more equitable distribution of incomes among rich and poor. The movement had a profound faith in Islam as the total blueprint for a modern society, and presented itself as an ideological and political alternative to liberalism or communism. It stripped away the traditional apparatus of Muslim learning and piety in favor of an almost Protestant-like devotion to the fundamentals of Islam and to reformist social and political programs. Committed to the fundamental scriptures of Islam, to the assertion of an Islamic social and political identity, and to the adaptation of Islamic principles to the needs of a modern society, the Muslim Brotherhood was devoted at once to the reform of morals, education, social and economic projects, and the creation of a Muslim state.

The Muslim Brotherhood failed in its bid for power, however. It was forestalled by the Free Officers' coup of July 1952 led by Naguib, Nasser, and Sadat. The new Egyptian regime was committed to a moderate form of authoritarian rule, centralized management of the economy, and a socialist ideology. In the 1950s and 1960s Nasser's regime attempted, as did the liberal regime of the 1920s, 1930s, and 1940s, to bypass the influence of Islam and pursue a secular policy. Strong government efforts were made to bring Islamic religious activity under government control. Opposition movements like the Muslim Brotherhood were outlawed, and the autonomy of other religious institutions was curtailed. Lands endowed for religious use were taken under government control in 1960 and 1973. Private mosques were also brought under government ministries. In 1961 the historic mosque-university al-Azhar was made a state university with a reformed curriculum. In the crucial field of legal administration, Muslim law courts were consolidated with the civil courts in 1955. Though the Muslim law continues to be applied, Muslim legal codes have been brought under governmental jurisdiction. In general, the government has tried to control religious life, to use the ulama to support government policy, and to identify Islam with national and socialist programs.

This effort to create an apparent identity of Islam and the state was only partially successful. Muslim sentiment in the country remains independent of state control. Just as the 1930s brought a revival of Islamic sentiments in intellectual and political circles, the 1970s has witnessed a revival of Islam appealing to middle class students and young professional people. There are several reasons for this revival of Islamic sentiment in Egypt. One is that deeply felt Islamic loyalties have not been eradicated but only held in abeyance among western-educated professional and governmental elites; they have not really been supplanted by new national, secular, or socialist loyalties. Second, while the ulama and the official Islamic establishment remain under government control, independent preachers, missionaries, and teachers actively promote a revived commitment to Islam. Finally, the political and social atmosphere of the late 1960s and 1970s has given a new cachet to religious loyalties. The 1967 defeat in the war with Israel revived the traditional Muslim view that defeat is due to lack of piety and commitment to Islam. At the same time, Egyptian failures in international politics, the failure to solve the Palestinian problem, and the failure to develop economically have led to condemnation of its secular and socialist policies. As Egyptians return to their faith for consolation, the government has been obliged to express its respect for Islam. Sadat himself took up the rhetoric of Islam and thereby lent added respectability to the new sentiment.

The problems of particular milieus have given these national issues increased relevance to important groups of people. Rapid urbanization of Cairo has brought previously small town or rural populations, without any sense of social or moral security, to a chaotic environment. Expansion of the educational system has created a large and growing class of students and university graduates without prospect of employment. Finally, the failures of the national, socialist, and secular regime is contrasted with the successes of regimes in such countries as Saudi Arabia and Iran where there is a revived importance of Islam. The result has been a return, especially among students and youth, to Islamic religious commitments in place of the secularist and socialist views of their parents' generation.

The new sentiment is the basis of the proliferation of Islamic revivalist groups. Generally speaking, these groups hold the same religious and social views as the Muslim Brotherhood. They believe that the Qur'an must be the basis of both individual morality and a just society, and they stress the application of Muslim law in all relevant matters. In social policy they hold that the primary role of women should be the care of the family. They stress the importance of individual moral behavior in economic life, while favoring lessening the differences in wealth between rich and poor and the creation of a mixed economy. For them, social justice is more important than technological, economic, or administrative issues. In general, these revivalist groups believe that their society has been corrupted by secular values and that only return to Islamic principles will restore morality, economic well-being, and political power.

This prescription leads some into terrorism. The Islamic Liberation Organization and the Repentance and Higra* group, who decry moral corruption and the acceptance of Western values, seek to change the society by first destroying the corrupt leadership. They have attempted assassinations of Egyptian political leaders in 1973 and 1977, and in 1981 they (or others sharing their views) succeeded in killing Sadat.

Most Islamic-minded people, however, are primarily concerned with personal morality, family values, and cultural authenticity. The 1970s revival appeals especially to students and professional people—engineers, schoolteachers, and white-collar workers—often from rural backgrounds and from upwardly and geographically mobile, but socially conservative, families. They have moved to Cairo, where they find themselves, despite their high professional qualifications, alienated by the inadequate salaries and distressed by the moral corruption of a big city. They are beset by sexual tensions due to the unexpected stimulations of the city and are concerned about finding proper spouses. In particular, young women professional students have begun to wear Islamic dress which does not reveal the figure or expose hair and limbs. This new commitment to Islamic modesty comes precisely at a time when women are increasingly entering professional schools and public life. Between 1952 and 1976 the ratio of female to male students in the universities has risen from one in thirteen to one in two. For women who are now entering the public world dominated by men, the veil and the profession of an Islamic modesty are ways of recreating the traditional separation of the sexes among young people who are otherwise—through education, travel and public transport, enjoyment of public entertainment, and political activities—

*Higra refers to the emigration of the prophet and his companions from Mecca to Medina, and signifies the passage from pagan to Islamic beliefs and society.

thrown together. The adoption of Islamic dress implies unavailability and asexuality, and for young women from conservative rural families it serves as a way of controlling sexual confusion and protecting family values and marriage possibilities. Thus, while the Islamic revival in Egypt has important political aspects, its most striking feature is that it is a mechanism of adjustment for Muslim students to the complexities of the professional and social situation in an urban environment.

In Egypt, the main vehicle of resistance to the failures of secular governments, whether liberal or socialist, on the part of both the old-fashioned petite bourgeoisie and western-educated students and professionals exposed to the stress of a changing economy, society, and political system, is Islam. Islamic movements, however, make their greatest impact at the level of personal and social values, and have not succeeded in national politics. Egypt is governed by a secularized political elite which dominates the ulama without being able, as is the Turkish elite, to commit the state to a secularist policy. The result is permanent Islamic revival. In the 1930s and 1940s the Muslim Brotherhood stressed the anti-imperialist aspects of Islam because it saw the main enemy to be the British. In the 1950s and 1960s it stressed solidarity and justice in opposition to the corruption of the military regime. In the 1970s the new Islamic reform movements emphasize personal morality and family values in response to the stresses of a changing social order. In Egypt as opposed to Turkey, Islam remains the main vehicle of resistance to the state and its policies. The basic structures of Egyptian society are similar to those of Turkish society, but because of the more limited powers of the Egyptian political elite and the more limited degree of social and economic differentiation in Egypt, there is a standing conflict between the secularized state elite and their Islamic petit bourgeois and student opponents.

3. THE ARAB FERTILE CRESCENT STATES

The Arab fertile crescent countries, including Syria, Iraq, Jordan, and Lebanon, have a very different heritage from that of Turkey and

Egypt. While Turkey and Egypt have strong traditions of centralized states, these former Ottoman provinces historically were divided into numerous small districts ruled by strong tribal and other local communities which resisted government intervention. Ottoman suzerainty never created effective central government.

Moreover, the present group of Arab states is an arbitrary creation, carved out of the debris of the Ottoman empire and given artificial boundaries by the British and the French at the end of World War I. Most of these states were held as mandated territories until after World War II, when they became independent. In recent decades, Syria and Iraq have been ruled by nationalist and socialist regimes built upon the support of elite cadres of army officers and Ba'ath party ideologues. Jordan is ruled by a conservative military elite, while Lebanon, plunged in civil war, has been unable to maintain a cohesive government.

As in other former lands of the Ottoman empire, the dominant political trend is toward the formation of secular national states. The ulama have been largely removed from a leading position in public life. Secular legal and judicial institutions have replaced the Muslim law. The decline of Muslim legal principles and the substitution of new law codes and court systems is perhaps the single most important index of the disestablishment of Islam in the public life of Arab countries.

In the Arab fertile crescent countries, the quest for national identity and the struggle for political power has for over a century been conducted in terms of Arab nationalism. Arabism has become the dominant discourse, displacing the traditional Islamic vocabulary of political affiliation and political action. Arab nationalism was born before World War I in the literary revival of the Arabic language, the revival of Arab identification with the glories of the Islamic past, and the anti-Turkish political ambitions of Arab intellectuals. Arab nationalism reached its first major political expression in the effort to establish an Arab state under the leadership of King Faysal at the end of World War I.

In the 1920s and 1930s the doctrine of Arab nationalism was extended beyond the realm of politics. On the theoretical and philosophical level, Arab nationalist thinkers tried to demonstrate the existence of an Arab nation and to define its moral, cultural, and political identity. Arab national identity came to be defined in terms of a shared language, a shared history, and a shared culture which could inspire the sentiments of loyalty, allegiance, and solidarity that would overcome the division of Arab peoples by tribes, regions, religions, and states. Sati al-Husri, an Iraqi Arab nationalist and educator, preached the need for unity and willingness to sacrifice parochial interests to the cause of the nation as a whole.

For Arab nationalist thinkers, nationalism was far more than patriotism. They defined it by the Arab word *qawmiya*, which means "belonging to a group," and implies a total absorption of the individual in the nation. Only through the nation can individuals achieve true freedom and a higher mode of existence. In the 1950s Michel Aflaq, the founder of the Ba'ath party, taught that through solidarity and love of the nation, Arab peoples would not only realize their political objectives but attain the highest spiritual fulfillment:

> The nationalism for which we call is love before everything else. It is the very same feeling that binds the individual to his family, because the fatherland is only a large household, and the nation a large family. Nationalism, like every kind of love, fills the heart with joy and spreads hope in the soul; he who feels it would wish to share with all the people this joy which raises him above narrow egoism, draws him nearer to goodness and perfection. . . . It is, then, the best way to a true humanity. . . .

> Nationalism is spiritual and all-embracing, in the sense that it opens its arms to and spreads its wings over all those who have shared with the Arabs their history and have lived in the environment of their language and culture for generations, so that they have become Arab in thought and feeling. There is no fear that nationalism will clash with religion, for, like religion, it flows from the heart and issues from the will of God; they walk arm in arm, supporting each other.*

*Quoted in Sylvia G. Haim, ed., *Arab Nationalism: An Anthology* (Berkeley, 1976), pp. 242-43.

Here religion not only walks arm in arm with nationalism, but has been absorbed into it. This kind of nationalism is a new faith which is expected to bring into being not only government but also justice, brotherhood, and love. As a faith it brings into politics a yearning for total security, total victory of good over evil, justice, and human fulfillment. Nationalism carries with it a religious yearning for salvation.

Arab nationalism then was a philosophy and a faith, but it served ideological as well as spiritual purposes. In the interwar years Arab nationalism was in practice a doctrine of opposition to foreign rule. After World War II, Arab identity became the basis of political goals such as anti-imperialism, struggle against Israel, and the formation of political regimes. Since the 1950s the two crucial themes in Arab nationalist thinking have been the struggle for unity and socioeconomic development. At this stage some form of socialism, communism, or Islam becomes a crucial aspect of Arab nationalist ideologies.

In Syria and Iraq, Arab nationalism stands in an ambivalent relation to state nationalisms. The Ba'ath party, which rules in both countries, espouses Arab unity, but separate wings of the party govern the two states and are deeply hostile to each other. Each regime in practice identifies Arab nationalism with the fulfillment of the socialist goals of its own state. A similar ambiguity characterizes the nationalism of the Palestinian movement. At one level it is a regional nationalism, yet it appeals to pan-Arab loyalties for political support. Some branches of the Palestinian movement see the ultimate solution to the Palestinian problem as the absorption of Palestine into a united Arab socialist society.

In the 1950s pan-Arabism became the banner of opposition to the elites of Syria, Iraq, and Jordan, and in the minds of secular pan-Arab nationalists and certain wings of the Palestinian movement, it has remained the banner of opposition to conservative regimes and foreign influence in Jordan, Saudi Arabia, and other conservative states.

Despite the disestablishment of Islam in the former Ottoman provinces and the dominance of Arab nationalist sentiment, Islam

31

still plays a substantial role in the identity of Arab peoples. This role is largely cultural. Arab national consciousness is still bound up with the historic identification of Arab peoples with Islam. Arab nationalist thinkers of the 1920s and 1930s stressed the virtual identity of Arabism and Islam. Islam they took to be the confirmation of the existence of an Arab nation—a religious expression of the national genius. The ideals of Islam were the ideals of the Arab nation; Muhammad was regarded as its founding father. Even Christian writers considered Arabism and Islam two expressions of the same identity; they stressed the glory of Muhammad as an heroic leader and praised his contribution to Arab nationality, but they maintained that national ties should transcend religious ties and advocated the formation of secular states. In the 1950s Abd al-Rahman al-Bazzaz, an Iraqi Arab nationalist writer and politician, argued that there was no contradiction between Arabism and Islam because both embodied the collective principles of the Arab nation. Many Arab nationalist thinkers found it impossible to distinguish between Arabism and Islam. The vocabulary of Arab nationalist thinking is infused with words such as *umma* (brotherhood of Muslims) and *milla* (religious community), which have strong religious overtones but are used to express national solidarity. Arab nationalist writers have borrowed the Islamic mystical concept of *fana'*—the idea of the loss of self and union with the divine being—to express the bond of the individual to the nation.

The common people follow the nationalist thinkers in identifying the Arab nation with Islam. For them, to be an Arab is still primarily to be a Muslim, to share in the revelation of the Qur'an and the glory of the Arab conquests. The rhetoric may be nationalist, but the emotional identifications are still Islamic. Most Muslim Arabs still have faith in the excellence of Islam, revere the Qur'an, and venerate Muhammad as an ideal human being. In this loyalty there is a strong instinct to defend Islam against Christianity and also a strong apologetic tendency to insist that Islam is a modern religion and a practical basis for a modern society.

This implicit identification of Arabism with Islam has important political as well as cultural implications. Islamic sentiment was crucial in the mobilization of Palestinians in the 1920s and 1930s to resist British rule and Zionism, and the Muslim attachment to Jerusalem remains important in Arab and Muslim world support for the Palestinian movement. Saudi support for the Palestinian cause, for example, does not distinguish Arab and Muslim interests.

Apart from being embedded in nationalism, militant Islamic resistance to established secular regimes has cropped up in several of the Arab fertile crescent countries. In Syria, the present Ba'ath regime, based on the support of the army, the Ba'ath party, the Alawis (a Muslim minority group), and other religious minorities, governs a majority Sunni Muslim population which is barely represented at the higher levels of government. Government policies tend to favor rural over urban populations, partly corresponding to the non-Sunni/Sunni split in political allegiances. Religiously defined Sunni opposition has surfaced in the form of the Muslim Brotherhood, founded in Aleppo and Damascus in the 1930s. As in Egypt the Muslim Brotherhood appeals to the "old bazaar" shopkeepers, artisans, craftsmen, and their modern educated student and intelligentsia offspring. Operating as a political party in the Syrian elections of 1961, the Muslim Brotherhood won 5.8 percent of the national vote and 17.6 percent of the Damascus vote. However, when Ba'ath party rule was consolidated in the 1960s and 1970s, the Muslim Brotherhood turned from electoral politics to civil disobedience and armed resistance. In the mid-1970s, in response to the Syrian government's intervention against the Palestinians in Lebanon, rising inflation, and the general decline of Sunni political influence, the Brotherhood launched guerrilla attacks and finally large-scale uprisings in Aleppo and Hama. These revolts were crushed by the regime, but it is too early to assess how well the Brotherhood will succeed in mobilizing Sunni support and in sustaining its opposition.

Ideological and militant opposition to the Ba'ath regime in Iraq has also emerged in the last few years. In the 1960s the Shi'a ulama formed the Da'wa al-Islamiya (Islamic Mission) to work for an Islamic state and social justice. The more militant Mujahidin or Muslim Warriors was founded in 1979. The relatively strong Iraqi regime, however, has reduced this opposition to sporadic terrorism. By contrast with Egypt, in neither Syria nor Iraq has Islam taken hold as a major expression of political and economic discontent.

In conclusion, Islam has been substantially disestablished in the public life of the fertile crescent countries and plays only a limited political role. It does not seem to be a major force in national politics, and organized political opposition, apart from the Muslim Brotherhood in Syria and sporadic Shi'a resistance in Iraq, does not usually adopt Islamic principles. In this region, however, Islam maintains a latent cultural significance. Despite a century-old commitment to secular forms of Arab nationalism, it remains an integral aspect of Arab identity.

4. IRAN

The role of Islam in Iran is altogether different than in Turkey, Egypt, and the Arab fertile crescent countries. The modern Iranian state was created by Reza Khan, later Shah, who came to power in 1925 and established a regime in the name of secular modernity and Persian nationalism. Reza Shah ruled in authoritarian fashion with the support of a small, upper-class stratum of landlords, soldiers, and westernized bureaucrats, and with strong foreign backing. For the first time in Iranian history, he built up a centralized army and administration, and laid the foundations for an industrial economy and for western-type educational and legal systems. Above all, he broke the power of Iran's tribal communities. The present Kurdish, Turkoman, and Baluchi resistance to revolutionary government is only the remnants of a once universal Iranian tribal structure.

Reza Shah was forced by the British to abdicate in 1941 and was replaced by his son Muhammad Reza Shah, who reigned until 1979. The first decade of his reign was a period of weak royal government and strong political parties, but after the Musaddeq period struggle over the nationalization of oil (1951-1953), the shah, with the aid of the army and covert American assistance, seized political power and suppressed both Musaddeq's national front and the Tudeh (Communist) party.

The restored regime of Muhammad Reza Shah was technically a constitutional regime, but the shah ruled with virtually absolute powers. He controlled the army, which was purged of leftists in the 1950s, selected the ministers and half of the senate, maintained a strong secret police, and manipulated elections to control the parliament.

In 1960 the shah launched the "White Revolution," a program of land reform that was bitterly opposed both by parliament and by the ulama, and was finally implemented by decree. In conjunction with the agricultural reforms, the shah proposed the formation of literacy and health corps, which were intended to be a political as well as a service cadre that would bring the direct influence of the government into the countryside. Other reforms included the extension of voting rights to women and their employment in government offices. In effect the shah's program called for the construction of a powerful centralized, secular, national regime and the modernization of economic, educational, and social life along western lines. It was essentially a continuation of the policies implemented by Reza Shah in the 1920s and 1930s which expanded the cadres of modern, western-educated intelligentsia, officials, soldiers, business managers, and skilled workers, and enlarged the modernized sector of the Iranian economy and society.

The shah's regime diminished the power of the ulama, but not decisively. Secular education, government supervision of religious schools, new legal codes, reductions of funds, and other measures for a time brought the ulama under state control. Measures were taken to ban passion plays, pilgrimages, and sermons, and to introduce new dress codes to symbolize the modernization of the country. The ulama, however, remained potentially powerful because of the veneration in which they were held, their close ties to the common people, their nationwide system of communication, and their history of opposing state policies.

Throughout this period the position of the ulama was ambiguous. The politically open years of the 1940s had encouraged ulama activism in political affairs, and from 1948 to 1953 Ayatullah Kashani, supported by street preachers and lower-ranking ulama, agitated for the nationalization of oil and the termination of foreign influence in Iran. For a time he supported the Mussadeq government.

The overthrow of Mussadeq in 1953, however, introduced a period of quietism and collaboration with the state authorities. The government lent tacit support to ulama interests, including appointments at court and opportunities for enrichment through landowning and marriage into prominent families. The government also supported ulama interests by suppressing the Baha'i, though not to the degree the clergy would have wished. The government increased the amount of religious instruction in public schools and periodically closed down movie houses, liquor stores, and public musical entertainments. In return, the ulama accepted the Baghdad Pact* and tolerated the government's policy of cooperation with foreign oil companies. Under the leadership of Ayatullah Burujirdi, the ulama maintained their political quiet but also consolidated their strength, and in the 1950s and early 1960s developed a national network of communications with Qum as the center of Shi'a religious instruction and organization.

The White Revolution caused a break in this cooperative relationship. The government's social and economic planning raised ulama concerns about the strengthening of state authority, and aroused their hostility to the particular measures proposed. They opposed the implementation of the new land laws, the extension of suffrage to women, and cooperation with Israel, and they felt threatened by the government's proposal to establish a literacy corps, which they feared would provide the state with cadres that could rival ulama influence in rural areas. The quarrel between the government and the ulama reached a climax in 1963 when the shah decided to call a national referendum on land reform. The proposed referendum and a police crackdown on ulama activities in Qum provoked demonstrations in opposition to the shah's rule and his relations with the United States and Israel. These demonstrations were led by Ayatullah Khumayni, who was exiled to Iraq in 1964. In 1970 there was yet another outburst of public protest against Iranian agreements with American business corporations.

*A mutual defense treaty signed by Iran with Turkey, Iraq, Great Britain, and Pakistan in 1955, in which the United States participated as an observer.

As important as renewed ulama resistance to the state authority was the development of a reform movement within ulama circles. The reformers urged the ulama to take a politically active role. Mihdi Bazargan in 1962 argued that collective struggle for a better society was the responsibility of the clergy: no longer should they wait passively for a return of the Messiah, but actively prepare the way. The reformers further proposed a comprehensive internal reorganization of the ulama, the formation of a governing council, and the creation of a centralized financial organization to assure the autonomy of the ulama from both government influences and popular pressures.

Between 1967 and 1973 the religious reform movement took a new direction under the leadership of Dr. Ali Shari'ati, who formed the Husayniyah Irshad. This was a kind of free university intended to revitalize Islam by reconciling Islamic teachings with European social sciences. Shari'ati taught that Shi'ism was a religion of protest, and thereby hoped to generate the commitment needed to overthrow a repressive government. At about the same time Muslim guerrilla groups, including the Mujahidin-i Khalq, began terrorist activities.

Ayatullah Khumayni, from his sanctuary in Iraq, became the main spokesman of opposition to the monarchy. In 1961 Khumanyi favored a constitutional monarchy, but by 1971 he had changed his mind. On the basis of the principles of *jihad* and "commanding the good," he argued that the clergy must resist a despotic government; in his book *Islamic Government* he attacked dynastic succession as un-Islamic and proposed a regime under ulama leadership with a parliament that had an "agenda setting" function. It was the most radical Iranian statement of ulama responsibilities ever formulated.

This revival of Islamic religious and political consciousness centered around ulama, intellectuals, students, and politicians soon became a movement of mass opposition to the regime of the shah. In the course of the 1970s, the shah's regime became even more oppressive. The army and the secret police were widely feared and hated for their widespread investigations of alleged enemies of the regime, which often involved intimidation, imprisonment, torture, or even execution. The regime was widely perceived as based upon American political and military support for the benefit of only a very narrow elite. It was not only hated for being a dictatorship but also was resented for mismanaging the economy. Great fortunes were being earned from oil income and were being spent on complex new weapons for the benefit of the military while inflation was undermining the standard of living of the industrial workers and the bazaar merchants, artisans, and laborers. The bazaar population suffered particularly from confiscations, fines, and imprisonment as the shah sought to contain inflation by intimidating the merchants. At the same time the 1970s was disastrous for the masses of Iranian peasants. They had not benefitted substantially from the land reform, and millions fled the land for the cities, where they formed a huge mass of unemployed and underemployed people. In the late 1970s, Iran was importing most of its food.

In these deeply disturbed political and economic conditions, a coalition of radical guerrilla groups, liberal politicians, and ulama was able to mobilize mass support for a series of demonstrations that eventually brought down the shah's regime. The revolution abolished the Iranian monarchy and established an Islamic government in Iran. Today, as the revolution proceeds, the most radical religious elements in the coalition which backed Khumayni's rise to power are eliminating their rivals.

5. PAKISTAN

Islamic revival in Pakistan differs profoundly from that in Turkey, the Arab world, and Iran. Pakistan is the only contemporary Muslim state to be founded in the name of Islam. In 1947 Britain gave up the government of India and partitioned its Indian empire into the Muslim state of Pakistan (which included Bangladesh until 1971) and the state of India. The Muslim nation of Pakistan was originally founded in the territories of Sind, Baluchistan, Northwest Frontier Provinces, west Punjab and east Bengal—a nation of some 80 million people in two great territorial blocks divided by a thousand miles of Indian soil. Some 50 million Muslims remained in India. The new nation was born in the throes of one of the most terrible civil and communal wars in modern history.

Despite its Muslim identity the new state of Pakistan was divided by profound ethnic and regional differences. In the western part of the country, more than half of the people were Punjabis, but some 20 percent were Sindhis, 13 percent Pathans, and 3-4 percent Baluchis. Bengal, separated by a thousand miles of Indian territory, was virtually a nation within the nation.

The country was also beset by grave economic and social problems. The western region was without industrial infrastructure, and the eastern region had been cut off from Calcutta, its main port and processing center for jute and other agricultural products. The upheavals of partition had led to the emigration or destruction of the non-Muslim trading and commercial classes in the west and landed elites in the east. From the Muslim point of view, the main problem of the state was to create a national identity to match the reality of the new political boundaries and to create an acceptable and stable regime for a populace divided by myriad ethnic, linguistic, and ideological distinctions, and even by religious differences over the role of Islam in the constitution of the new state.

Pakistan came into being with two widely held, divergent concepts of what was meant by an Islamic state. The political elite considered Islam a communal and national identification only—a political identity stripped of religious content. But a large segment of the populace, led by the ulama and other religious leaders, believed the new state should be dedicated to the formation of a society whose constitution, institutions, and routines of daily life were governed by Islamic law.

At the outset the pressure for the formation of a religious state was very great. Muhammad Ali Jinnah, the first president of Pakistan, agreed that its institutions should not be in conflict with Muslim law. The assembly called to draft a constitution for the new state agreed that it must have an Islamic framework, and established a Board of Islamic Teaching to advise on the religious aspects of the new constitution. This board recommended that the state be governed by pious Muslim leaders in accord with the advice of the ulama. The pressures exerted by popular religio-political movements were also great. One of the most powerful of these was the Jama'at-i Islami, led by Adu'l A'la Mawdudi, a Muslim reformer, fundamentalist, and political organizer, who was strongly committed to the transformation of Pakistan into a Muslim state. Mawdudi held that sovereignty is possessed by God, and that His law must prevail. He believed that the purpose of the state was to enforce Muslim law and to mold its citizens according to the norms of Islam. Mawdudi opposed Western nationalist principles. He also opposed the legal teaching of the conventional ulama, and appealed for a return to the basic principles of the Qur'an and the sayings of the prophet, making use of rational judgment so as to apply these principles in a way consistent with the demands of modern society. The Jama'at movement insisted that governing officials be advised by religious councils and that non-Muslims be barred from high political posts. In 1956 the first constitution of Pakistan declared it an Islamic state.

While the debates over the constitution went on, the real government of Pakistan was a Punjabi elite of soldiers, administrators, and landowners. After ten years of chaotic civilian rule, the question of the role of Islam had not been resolved, and the ethnic and regional rivalries between West Pakistan and Bengal persisted. In 1958 the army, led by General Ayyub Khan, took control of the country. His government was highly centralized and strongly supported by landlords, business interests, and government officials, as well as by the Sufi custodians of popular shrines. On the Islamic issue, the new regime followed its predecessor's policy of making formal gestures toward Islam. In the Constitution of 1962 it created an Advisory Council of Islamic Ideology, and called for the compatibility of government legislation with the Qur'an and the teachings of the prophet, but it also upheld the principle of religious freedom. The constitution banned political parties, and thus weakened the Jama'at-i Islami, which had been the leading force for religious influence in government affairs.

General Ayyub Khan's regime began to fail in 1965. Defeat in war with India led to demands for a reopening of the electoral system, and the Bengalis demanded provincial autonomy. Demonstrations and riots led in 1969 to the succession of General Yahya Khan, who imposed martial law and precipitated a struggle that led eventually to another war with India and the formation of east Pakistan into the independent state of Bangladesh in 1971.

The question of the relationship of the religious and political aspects of Islam remains unresolved. From 1970 to 1977 [West] Pakistan was under the leadership of Zu'lfiqar Ali Bhutto and the Pakistan People's Party, which espoused an Islamic socialism compounded of agricultural and industrial reforms and the promulgation of a new constitution that defined Pakistan as an Islamic republic. The president and prime minister were to be Muslims, and all laws were to be in conformity with Islam as determined by a council of ulama. Bhutto advocated an Islamic socialism in reaction to the nationalist and regionalist tensions that were tearing Pakistan apart, but partly in deference to vested business interests, and partly in deference to aid from Arab countries, he progressively moved from emphasis upon socialism to emphasis upon Islam, and introduced such moral reforms as the outlawing of drinking and gambling.

In 1977 Bhutto was overthrown by a military coup led by General Zia ul-Haq, who introduced Islamic criminal punishments, abolished English as the main language of school instruction, and created a new institution for the application of Muslim religious law attached to the Pakistani supreme court. The new regime's strong commitment to Islam, under the influence of the Jama'at-i Islami, which calls for the creation of an Islamic political system, Islamic banking, and Islamic taxation, suggests an almost desperate need to legitimate an unpopular government.

Pakistan then was formed out of a deep conviction that Muslims in India required a state of their own to assure their political security and their right to cultivate a Muslim style of life, but since its founding the state has not been able to resolve the question of what kinds of institutions Pakistan should have or overcome the ethnic and social divisions in the country. Strong groups such as Punjabi landlords and bureaucrats, Pathan tribal chiefs, and ethnic minorities have put their interests ahead of those of the nation as a whole. There have been a number of constitutions, and both civilian and military regimes. The country holds together by military coercion, by strong administration, and by bargaining among various groups, but not by any deep sense of national identity. The political and military elites continue, as in 1947, to appeal to Islam to overcome the inherent divisions of the country. In Pakistan, in contrast to Iran, the Islamic revival has politically conservative implications.

IV

ANALYSIS: CULTURE AND POLITICS IN ISLAMIC COUNTRIES

While the Islamic revival is a worldwide development, its specific manifestations and relative importance vary from country to country. To better understand the various movements, we must analyze them in two dimensions: first, in terms of the way Islamic beliefs, symbols, and values serve to mobilize social and political action; second, in terms of how Islamic movements and political action operate in particular national contexts.

RELIGION AND POLITICAL ACTION

The Islamic movements in the present revival represent several types. One of them (and the most potent)—the Iranian revolution—is *sui generis*. It is grounded in the existence of an organized nationwide religious establishment, closely in touch with the common people, enabled by virtue of the historical weakness of Iranian states to represent the conscience and economic interests of the populace in opposition to state policies. The revolution in Iran grows out of an historic religious establishment capable—both for distinctive Shi'a religious and doctrinal reasons and because of special Iranian political circumstances—of actively opposing the political regime.

The others are Sunni movements. Some are based on the Sufi reformist movements which trace back to the eighteenth and nineteenth centuries. The revived Naqshbandi activity in Turkey and Central Asia, the Deoband colleges in Pakistan and India, the Muhammadiya in Indonesia, and others echo an old tradition. Their basic concern is the cultivation of an intellectual and spiritual practice of

43

Islam based on the teachings of the Qur'an and the prophet, and the repudiation of saint worship and other practices which have become common anong Muslim peoples but which they do not consider intrinsically Islamic. These movements espouse moral reform, educational improvement, and social activism, and oppose foreign influences and colonial intervention. Their basic impulse remains, however, religious purity.

Most of the organized Islamic movements in the Middle East and Pakistan derive only indirectly from previous reform and scripturalist tendencies. They are "neo-Muslim," led by preachers and teachers, such as Hasan al-Banna of the Muslim Brotherhood or Mawdudi of the Jama'at-i Islami, who are not themselves ulama or Sufis in the traditional or reformist sense, though they may have some traditional education. Moreover, these religious leaders are founders of a new type of religious organization—no longer based on traditional schools of law or Sufi brotherhoods, but based on study groups, scout groups, women's auxiliaries, athletic clubs, economic enterprises, political parties, and paramilitary units.

They also appeal to a new clientele: in part to the bazaar, or old middle-class elements, displaced by economic and political change, and in part to the modern educated technical intelligentsia. It is striking that, in Turkey, Islamic student groups and parties are strongest in the technical faculties while socialist groups predominate in the arts faculties. In Egypt, Islamic radicalism wins its strongest supporters among students in medicine, engineering, pharmacy, and other highly professional clienteles. In Iran, student leadership was crucial in the internal Islamic revival up until the revolution. The new classes of intelligentsia—socially mobile and educated military officers, administrators, engineers, technicians, journalists, lawyers, and industrial managers—are successful but unsatisfied people. Separated by their education from traditional communities, they are not really part of the political elite. While their education prepares them for high-level positions, they are often confined to marginal journalistic or bureaucratic jobs. Others, such as traders and artisans threatened with industrial competition, and landless peasants, are simply pushed to extinction. Families are upset as young people no longer accept the authority of their elders, and women insist upon or are required to adopt new roles in society and new relationships with men. Millions of people are affected: they are alienated from home, family, and religious community, and most are made dependent upon the state for protection, employment, welfare, and survival. For these reasons, Islamic movements appeal both to declining middle-class bazaar merchants and artisans and to their socially mobile but professionally and politically insecure children.

Furthermore, the neo-Muslim movements do not preach a traditional doctrine. Their religious appeal is not based on traditional Islamic teaching in law, theology, or mysticism. They are a new version of Islam using a generalized rhetoric which appeals to the conviction that Islam embraces the totality of human experience. In the words of Sayyid Qutb (1906-1966), an important Egyptian Muslim teacher:

> Above all other things it is a comprehensive human justice, and not merely an economic justice; that is to say, it embraces all sides of life and all aspects of freedom. It is concerned alike with the mind and the body, with the heart and the conscience. . . . Thus, in the Islamic view, life consists of mercy, love, help, and a mutual responsibility between Muslims in particular, and between all human beings in general.*

A pamphlet prepared by the Islamic Association of Cairo University entitled "Lessons from Iran," distributed in 1979, says of Islam:

> It is a comprehensive religion which legislates for this world and the next and organizes all of life. It is concerned with the justice of government just as it is concerned with assuring that prayer is performed. It sets up a system for economy of which zakāt [almsgiving] is a part. It establishes its society on bases of creed and equality among the people and the brotherhood of faith. It sets forth in detail rules for dealings between people just as it details

*John J. Donohue and John L. Esposito, *Islam in Transition* (New York, 1982), pp. 125-26.

the rules of worship. It organizes the relations between the Islamic state and other states. It is religion and state, governance and politics, economics and social organization, education and morals, worship and holy war.*

For the neo-Muslim movements, Islam is the design of a comprehensive and exalted way of life. In it is contained all individual and social goods. The rhetoric of these movements expresses a faith in Islam as a state of being in which virtue, human decency, and political security are realized. For the spokesmen and adherents of these movements, Islam symbolizes the utopian dream of a truly human, indeed divine, community; Islam is *communitas*, the Kingdom of God.

While their utopian aspirations have a basis in traditional Islamic beliefs, they go beyond the historical meaning of Islam. Traditionally, religion provided a faith and a community, but it played only a limited part in politics. States and empires were legitimated in religious terms, and were supposed to defend the religious interests of Muslims and uphold religious law, but religion's role was in fact quite limited. By contrast, the neo-Muslim movements take the deep psychological needs for faith and fellowship and project them into political causes. Religious belief, solidarity, and feeling are more and more channelled into politics, and political actions are more and more based on religious concepts and loyalties. In the modern era religious feeling becomes the basis of total commitments to nations and states, movements and causes. The merging of religion and politics may be a classic Islamic ideal, but only in the recent era are they actually being brought together.

Another important characteristic of all of these movements—Iranian Shi'a, Sufi reformist, and neo-Muslim—is that they express both personal religious and collective political goals in the same condensed symbols. They all link personal morality directly to political action. The Sufi reformist movements ordinarily begin by reaffirming the principles of personal religious belief and practice, and end up by

*Ibid., p. 247.

attempting to reform Muslim society as a whole and defend it against foreign colonial or corrupt (in their view) domestic political regimes. The neo-Muslim movements have been devoted from their very onset to conjoined individual and collective reform, which they see as indissolubly interrelated. In the 1960s the Iranian ulama began their political careers by rediscovering the political implications of their religious responsibility.

All these cases are based upon deeply rooted Muslim assumptions about the relation of religion and politics. As I have said elsewhere:

> For Muslims all economic and political problems are at bottom moral problems.... All varieties of traditional Muslim political literature, whether of the Sunni juristic, or philosophic, or "Mirror for Princes" type, focus on the personal goodness of the ruler as the basis of a good Muslim society. This is because a good society is not conceived in terms of institutions, but is understood to be the product of good character in the ruler leading to good deeds which restrain evil men and are an example for his subjects on how to be good themselves. Ethical writers are heartily in agreement. The basis of a good and powerful Muslim society is people with belief in Islam, virtuous impulses, and commitment to religious law. A good society stems ultimately from the goodness of men. Americans, on the contrary, tend to think that a well-run economic and political society is regulated by the legitimate competition of interests. Interest groups compete; lawyers, legislators, governors help to resolve their problems. Americans believe that the free, or at least regulated, competition of interests generates a healthy and powerful society. Traditional Muslim thought sees the competition of interests as immoral and government institutions to regulate and channel such competition as worse than useless. For Muslims a healthy, powerful, and just society stems from the good behavior of individuals, and the route to a just and powerful society is through the reform of the hearts and minds of men—through the practice of, and belief in, and commitment to Islam.... It is no accident that the term jihād applies at once to the inner struggle of

the soul for virtue and to the outer struggle for the political advantage of the Muslim community.*

The condensation of individual and political expectations in the same symbolic language allows reformist or neo-Muslim movements to operate across a broad spectrum of concerns. They preach individual morality; they espouse educational improvements and social welfare; and they aspire to control state economic policies and foreign affairs to realize Islamic goals. Such reform and revival movements are highly adaptable in that they can shift their goals from one level to another depending upon political circumstances. For example, in the 1940s, the Muslim Brotherhood in Egypt became increasingly politically oriented, but in the 1950s and 1960s it was able to restrict its public activities and go underground to continue its religious missionary work. Islamic fervor in Egypt surfaced again in the 1970s to work for both individual and social goals. Similarly, in other Muslim countries, Islamic movements wax and wane depending upon their opportunities. Another example is the Islamic movements in Indonesia, which attempted in the last decade of Dutch rule and in the early years of the independent Indonesian republic to win control of the state. When defeated in the elections of 1955 and by the subsequent assumption of power by Sukarno and the Indonesian army, they returned to their basic moral and educational activities.

The condensation of spiritual and political goals in the symbol of Islam also helps explain the almost protean adaptability of Islamic rhetoric to so many different political and social situations. Islam is used to oppose regimes and to defend them; it is sometimes conservative, sometimes revolutionary; sometimes nationalist, sometimes anticolonial; sometimes bourgeois reformist, sometimes the banner of student, peasant, tribal, worker, intellectual, professional, or military groups who call for radical and even revolutionary changes. Islam is sometimes pragmatic and sometimes millenarian. It bears a great variety of potential meanings for

*I. M. Lapidus, "Islam and the Historical Experience of Muslim Peoples," in *Islamic Studies: A Tradition and Its Problems*, ed. Malcolm H. Kerr (Malibu, 1980), p. 99.

it provides the symbols of loyalty, the rhetoric of identification, the justification of leadership, the rationale, the legitimation and the motivation for action. Islam as a religion, as a set of beliefs, [and as a political ideology] supplies the vocabulary and the images that Muslim peoples use to cope with mundane political, economic, and institutional problems. . . . Islamic beliefs constitute the vocabulary of political action, the elements of which may be combined and recombined in innumerable ways depending upon situational needs.*

ISLAM AND THE STATE

Thus on a psychological, religious, and cultural level, neo-Muslim and reformist movements share certain general features and reflect an Islamic cultural orientation toward political action. However, the actual political role of Islamic movements differs in different countries. While Iran is going through an Islamic revolution, in Pakistan the Islamic revival is sponsored by the state itself. In Egypt a secular, nationalist, and socialist state is opposed in Muslim terms by its own youth, whereas in Turkey the secular state can brush off a similar Islamic revival as but one of several political problems. These variations in the political role of Islam are reflections of the contexts in which Islamic movements operate and of profound historical differences in the long-term evolution of the several Islamic societies of the Middle East and South Asia. To understand the differences among Turkey, Egypt, the Arab countries, Iran, and Pakistan, we have to look back into history for the origins of the state, religious, and other (particularly tribal and ethnic) institutions which are critical in their contemporary situation. The historic development of these institutions and the variations in the several Muslim societies help explain the differences among them and the varied roles of Islamic movements in each. To attempt to account for these differences, we shall look in turn at (1) the Ottoman empire (c. 1280-1923), which is the

*Ibid., pp. 100-101.

ancestor of modern Turkey, Egypt, and the Arab states, (2) the Safa-vid (1500-1722) and Qajar (1779-1925) empires, the ancestors of modern Iran, and (3) the Mughal empire (1526-1857), the ancestor of modern Pakistan. We shall try to see how the institutional structures of these empires, and their transformations in the nineteenth and twentieth centuries, influenced the differing roles of Islamic move-ments in twentieth-century states.

For the purpose of discussion, let us assume that Middle Eastern and South Asian Islamic societies historically have been composed at base of small-scale, local communities unified by an embracing reli-gious affiliation—Islam—and subordinate to state regimes. In general the small communities were organized and identified in lineage, tribal, and ethnic terms. Islam was articulated at two levels—as a culture of beliefs and practices rooted in the consciousness of individuals, and in the form of particular religious institutions such as ulama schools of law and Sufi mystical brotherhoods. The political regimes were generally built on some combination of court, feudal, and bureau-cratic institutions, commonly included both Muslim and non-Muslim elites, and were legitimated in both Islamic and non-Islamic terms. Such institutions and the interactions among them governed the evolution of the Ottoman, the Safavid and Qajar, and the Mughal empires; the variations in the character of these institutions and in the pattern of their interaction help explain many of the differences among these empires and important aspects of their transformation in the nineteenth and twentieth centuries.

THE OTTOMAN EMPIRE AND TURKEY

In the Ottoman empire the historic relations of state, tribal, and religious institutions show a pattern that is crucial for what has happened to Turkey in the twentieth century. The Ottoman empire was created by migrating bands of Turkish-speaking warriors between the late thirteenth and the sixteenth centuries. At its greatest extent the empire included Anatolia (Turkey) and the Arab provinces of the Middle East and North Africa as far as Morocco. In Europe it extended as far north as the Ukraine and as far west as Austria. The empire was named after the ruling Ottoman dynasty. Before the twentieth century its elites spoke a highly literary version of Turkish, but did not consider themselves a "national" or "Turkish" elite. Instead they defined their identity in terms of loyalty to the ruling house—as Ottomans—and the common people defined themselves in lineage or tribal terms. Under the Ottoman dynasty the newly conquered empire was rapidly organized into a highly centralized regime based on a slave military elite (the Janissaries), a bureaucratic financial administration, and a Muslim religious administration. The Ottoman state was a highly legitimate regime: legitimate in Muslim terms as a warrior state (the Ottomans were the greatest Muslim conquerors of all time), legitimate as a sponsor and patron of Muslim religious life and of the Muslim law, and legitimate in terms of a non-Muslim cosmopolitan and imperial tradition which harked back to Turkish empires in Central Asia, to Islamic Middle Eastern empires, and to the Byzantine empire. This imperial culture consisted of patrimonial concepts of the sultan's authority, a state law apart from the Muslim law, and an artistic tradition in architecture, manuscript illumination, and other fields which were accepted as intrinsic to an Islamic state, but gave the Ottomans an alternative non-Muslim basis for legitimacy.

The Ottoman regime dominated Islamic religious life through an exceptionally elaborate bureaucratic organization. The Ottomans supported an extensive hierarchical system of colleges and a complex judicial administration. The ulama were paid by state salaries and endowments, and their careers were regulated by the two overlapping administrative hierarchies. The Sufis, who initially led migrating warrior bands that tried to resist Ottoman authority, were co-opted by Ottoman-endowed *tekkes* (hospices), attached to the Ottoman court and the army, and suppressed by reform-minded ulama. In these conditions the Sunni ulama were totally committed to the authority of the sultan and accepted a legacy of religious attitudes which legitimated the political order. They taught that even a corrupt regime had to be obeyed because, in their view, the alternative was anarchy and communal violence.

51

The regime also dominated its town, tribal, and non-Muslim populations. It regulated the urban economy through guilds, and the Christian population was held politically subordinate through the *millet* system, under which non-Muslim populations were administered through the agency of semi-autonomous church organizations. Only the rural populations escaped close Ottoman control. As early as the fourteenth and fifteenth centuries, the Ottoman state had defeated Turkish and Kurdish tribal principalities in Anatolia, and after 1517 forced Arab tribes in Syria and Egypt to accept Ottoman suzerainty. Still in the course of the sixteenth and seventeenth centuries, local chieftains, Sufis, and brigands continued to fight for autonomy. However, while tribal communities resisted state control, they did not challenge Ottoman authority and were not rivals for imperial political power.

Thus by the eighteenth century the Ottoman empire had an institutional order which emphasized a centralized state regime, legitimated in both Muslim and non-Muslim terms, and a centralized and unified Sunni religious establishment which served virtually as a department of state, wholly committed to the Ottoman regime. Despite sporadic rural resistance, through bureaucratic administration, millets, and guilds, the Ottoman regime controlled its subjects to a degree unparalleled in Iran and India.

The late eighteenth and nineteenth centuries brought important changes to Ottoman society which served to carry over the pattern of state domination of religious and tribal communities into the twentieth century. In the course of the eighteenth and nineteenth centuries, the Ottoman empire went through a period of decentralization of power and internal decline. Throughout the empire, *ayan* and *derebeys*, lords of the valleys, Bedouin chiefs, Janissary officers, and others were able to wrest power from the sultan. In the Christian parts of the Balkans, the growth of trade and the emergence of new landowning and merchant elites, autonomous peasant communities, and bandit gangs had still more drastic implications for the Ottoman regime by favoring new nationalist ideologies which further undermined the authority of the sultan and reduced the potentiality for any reconsolidation of Ottoman centralized government.

Equally important in the Ottoman decline was the intervention of foreign powers, especially Russia and Britain, who encroached on Ottoman territory, took control of Ottoman trade, and began to influence the cultural values of Ottoman society. The foreign powers did not take direct control of the empire, as the British did in India or the Dutch in Indonesia, but they nonetheless undermined the Ottoman regime. First, they set in train a process which stripped the Ottoman empire of its non-Muslim and then of its non-Turkish-speaking populations. In the nineteenth century, Balkan peoples rebelled against Ottoman rule and established independent states in Greece, Serbia, Bulgaria, and Roumania. World War I completed the dismemberment of the Ottoman empire by detaching the Arab provinces. Also in the course of World War I and its aftermath, the Turkish elites destroyed the Armenian population of eastern Anatolia (1916), expelled invading Greek armies (1922), and crushed Kurdish resistance (1925) to create a relatively homogeneous national society. Thus tribal, ethnic, and national minorities were not a barrier to the formation of a Turkish national state. Where tribal and ethnic minorities remained part of the political system, the formation of modern states, as in Iran and the Indian subcontinent, took place on very different terms.

The second consequence of foreign pressure was to provoke the state elites to attempt to save the empire by modernizing it along western lines—by improving military capabilities, rationalizing administration, restoring the authority of the central government, and making the social and cultural changes necessary to support a centralized state. The Ottoman elite reformed the millets and introduced new legal codes and a new educational system. These administrative and educational reforms brought into being a new kind of intelligentsia—the graduates of military, medical, engineering, and diplomatic schools—who in each successive generation espoused a still more radical program of reform.

By 1860 a "Young Ottoman" intelligentsia turned from questions of technical and political reforms to the modernization of Islam, which they held—properly understood—was compatible with a modern society and a constitutional government. They promoted the use of a simplified version of Turkish to help bridge the gap between the Ottoman elite and the masses of their subjects. After 1900 a still more radical "Young Turk" generation gave up Islam altogether and turned toward a more secular and national concept of Turkish society. By World War I the ruling Committee of Union and Progress was committed to Turkish domination and secularization in place of Ottomanism and Islam. The parts of this elite that survived the defeats of World War I, under the leadership of Mustafa Kemal, restored their legitimacy by the successful expulsion of European occupation forces and the Greeks. They came to power confident of their authority and emboldened by their victories to embark on a radical cultural and economic transformation of Turkish society.

The Ottoman religious elites could offer no effective response either to European intervention or to the determination of the state elites to create a secular national state. The religious elites were in effect subordinate functionaries of the state, committed to the authority of a regime which for centuries had been a warrior state and protector of Muslim peoples. Throughout the nineteenth century, Ottoman sultans continued to stress their credentials as caliphs and defenders of Islam. With their base of power crushed by the liquidation of the Janissaries in 1826, and ambivalent about reform because of their desire to see a revitalization of Muslim life, the ulama were unable to resist the program of the state intelligentsia. Whatever the opinion of the ulama, and whatever the shock to the feelings of masses of Turkish Muslims, the voice of the westernized political establishment was the only one heard at the foundation of the Turkish republic.

Thus, from its inception the Turkish republic was aggressively committed to cultural revolution and to state-sponsored economic development. The heritage of strong state control, the nineteenth-century circumstances which turned the political elites to western-type reforms, and the subordination of the religious establishment allowed the state elites to pursue policies of economic and cultural development that seem to have broken the inherited institutional pattern and created a more differentiated and pluralistic society. Thus, in Turkey, we have seen that the Islamic revival takes place in a context of strong state control and pluralistic ideological and economic competition.

IRAN

Iran has a very different history of relations among tribal, religious, and state institutions and thus a different contemporary situation. The nomadic invasions of the eleventh to the fourteenth centuries established a large Turkish-speaking tribal population that shifted the demographic, ecological, and political balances of Iranian society in favor of Turkish-speaking nomadic or semi-nomadic peoples as opposed to Iranian peasants. The Turkish and Mongol migrations also introduced the Central Asian *uymaq* (extended household) as the basis of Iranian political life. The whole of Iran was parcelled out under control of chieftains supported by their families and client groups who dominated peasants and town populations from which they exacted tribute. A coalition of such uymaq chieftains under the leadership of the Safavid family conquered Iran in 1500 and established a dynasty that lasted until 1722. The Safavids were succeeded by yet another uymaq state—the Qajar (1779-1925). Ever since the beginning of the sixteenth century, then, Iran has been ruled by regimes that were weakly centralized and had little political power. The shahs of Iran have scarcely ever been more than suzerains over a society that was actually controlled by numerous tribal lords and their followers.

The relations between Iranian regimes and the religious establishment have been variable. The Safavid regime totally dominated the ulama of Iran just as the Ottomans dominated their ulama. Safavid authority was based on the claim that they were the true *imams* (successors of the prophet and religious leaders of all Muslims) and chiefs of an elite religious movement which claimed absolute obedience from its followers. The Safavids converted Iran to Shi'ism, made it the official religion, and created a monolithic religious establishment. They built up cadres of ulama, especially from Iraq, and suppressed rival Sunni and Shi'a movements. Official Shi'ism absorbed Sufi gnostic philosophy and popular saint worship, and Iran took on a religious homogeneity unknown in either the Ottoman or the Mughal empires. The ulama depended upon the state for political support, and benefitted from state appointments to offices and endowments for shrines. In return they legitimized and supported the central government against its tribal rivals. Thus the Safavid pattern of institutions was marked by a highly legitimate but weakly centralized state, a strong but subordinate religious establishment, and very strong but insubordinate tribal principalities.

That pattern was altered in the eighteenth and nineteenth centuries. The Safavid regime was succeeded by the Qajar, which governed Iran for 150 years, but was never able to effectively control the country, and maintained its position by exploiting the rivalries among the various local chiefs. This regime was also weakened by Russian and British territorial and economic encroachments, and came to depend upon foreign support and the competition among foreign powers for its existence. By contrast with the Ottoman empire, western intervention neither stripped away tribal or ethnic minorities nor provoked any effective westernization and reform.

While the Qajar regime was in decline, the power of the religious establishment was enhanced. In the course of the nineteenth century, the ulama of Iran vastly enlarged the religious authority of the Mujtahids (interpreters of religious law), organized a nationwide system of communication, and consolidated their ties with the common people through social and religious services. All of this led to the construction of a politically autonomous and nationwide religious community that one might call a church but for the lack of a formal hierarchy. The ulama, however, remained divided among those who actively asserted Islamic interests and those who were politically passive, and those who were favored with state grants of land and those who were not so favored.

By the end of the century the state and the religious establishment were in conflict over the increasing economic power of Russian and British interests. The ulama and other intelligentsia organized mass protests against the government's surrender to foreign pressures. These confrontations culminated in 1891-1892 in protests against a tobacco monopoly granted British financiers, and in the constitutional revolution of 1906, which led to the creation of a short-lived parliamentary regime. The historical weakness of the state and the autonomy of religious, tribal, and other local communities made it possible to organize a revolutionary movement under Islamic auspices. Iranian history in the twentieth century, as we have seen, repeated the conflict of state and religion, but changed the role of tribal and ethnic communities. Reza Shah broke the power of the tribal communities, but ulama opposition led, as in 1906, to the formation of a national coalition which overthrew the regime.

In the Ottoman empire, the state elites, who were committed by nineteenth-century changes to a secular concept of a society and did not (after World War I) have to contend with serious tribal or ethnic opposition, dominated the religious elites and created a modern Turkish state in their own ideological image. In Iran, by contrast, the weakened state inherited from the nineteenth century, due partly to the strength of tribal communities, allowed for the consolidation of a religious establishment capable of opposing state power. In the twentieth century, the elimination of tribalism as a crucial third force led to a polarization between the state and the general society led by the ulama. Thus in the Ottoman empire the historical strength of the state and subordination of the religious establishment allowed the state elites to govern the direction of twentieth-century development, while in Iran the historic weakness of the state and the potential autonomy of the religious establishment allowed for national revolutionary struggle in the name of Islam.

THE MUGHAL EMPIRE AND THE INDIAN SUBCONTINENT

The evolution of modern Pakistan has been based upon the interactions of state, religious, tribal, and ethnic institutions embedded in the Mughal empire, which reigned over the Indian subcontinent from 1526 to 1857. The Mughal state, unlike the Ottoman and the Safavid empires, had a mixed Muslim and non-Muslim elite and ambiguous cultural credentials. The political elite included Afghan,

Iranian, and Central Asian Muslim soldiers and native non-Muslim vassals. The aristocracy of the empire was defined in patrimonial and lineage as well as in Muslim terms. The empire was legitimized both as a patron and defender of Muslim religious life and as the bearer of a culture in which painting, music, literature, philosophy, and architecture embodied an Indian as well as a Muslim heritage. From the Mughal point of view, the political regime was a condominium of lineages bound to the emperor by territorial or political concessions, family ties, religious ideology, and cultural style.

Muslim society under Mughal rule was exceedingly diverse. The Muslims of India did not constitute a single community, but comprised different groups representing many classes of population, lineages, and even castes. Some were warrior elites descended from the Mughals, Turks, and Afghans who had conquered India; others were *sayyids* (descendants of the prophet Muhammad); some were scholarly and scribal lineages who traced their descent to Persian and Arab Muslim notables. Still others were not descended from foreign-born elites, but were converts who kept their occupations and their familial and territorial names. Thus the religious situation of the subcontinent differed from the Ottoman and Iranian situations because there was no dominant concept of Islam and no single Muslim community or religious establishment. Indian Muslims formed many religious bodies—some Sunni, some Shi'a—further divided by allegiance to *jamatbandis* (religious communities), schools of law, Sufi brotherhoods and shrines of saints, and to the teachings of individual scholars and holy men. Intense religious debates among the law-minded and the theosophical and shrine-oriented Sufis, along with the conflicts between reformers and devotees of Indian popular religious practices, gave Indian Islam an unparalleled vitality.

The relation of the Mughal empire to Muslim religious life was conditioned by this pluralism. Though the state patronized a small ulama establishment, both ulama and Sufis were generally independent. Reformist-minded ulama who represented a universalistic Islamic ideal were often critical of the non-Muslim aspects of the Mughal state, its cosmopolitan and imperial culture, its Hindu elite, and its patrimonial loyalties. In some areas, however, the Sufi religious leaders became a shrine- and land-controlling gentry with an important political role mediating between the state and their clients. They tended to accept state support and the legitimacy of the regime, but managed to elude state control.

In the eighteenth and nineteenth centuries, the Mughal empire was overwhelmed by foreigners. Unlike the more resilient Ottoman and Qajar empires, it was utterly destroyed and replaced by the British empire. There was no continuing Muslim state to channel the further development of the society and no organized religious establishment to speak for its values. Rather, a multi-sided struggle broke out among Muslims, as well as with regional non-Muslim powers, including the Marathas, Sikhs, Jats, and the British, over the political and cultural future of India.

The Muslims took several positions reflecting the pluralistic class, religious, and ethnic structure of Mughal society. The old Muslim bureaucratic and landowning lineages accommodated to the reality of British rule and tried to maintain the position of their class. The Mughal political elite adopted a western type of education, and espoused a modernized Islamic religion to make it consistent with the technical, cultural, and political order of the times. Out of this milieu came Aligarh, the premier Indian Muslim college and later university, whose graduates in succeeding generations were the main supporters of the Muslim League. By the 1930s the Muslim League demanded political guarantees for the security of the Muslim minorities in the form of a separate Muslim electorate and regional autonomy. By 1938 the leaders of the Muslim League claimed that there were two nations in India—one Hindu, one Muslim—by virtue of the differing religious and cultural heritages; in 1940 the League resolved that the Muslim nation must have a separate homeland, a state of its own—Pakistan.

The demand for a separate Muslim state marked a revolution in Muslim thought. The League emphasized Islam as a political identity rather than as a religion. Its program was that of a secularized elite of landowners, officeholders, politicians, and journalists who were not necessarily committed to the religious tradition, but were forced by competition with the majority Hindu population, combined with the deep-rooted ethnic, tribal, and local differences among Muslims, to espouse an Islamic form of nationalism as a unifying symbol. Similarly, because the British had held India together rather than allowing it to break into particularistic states, as in the Ottoman empire, the secularized Muslim political elites were obliged to use an Islamic ideology to rally the support of co-religionists in their struggle with the British and with non-Muslim elites and communities.

The Muslim religious leaders attempted to reconstruct Muslim society, stressing the religious aspects of Islam—the rational, disciplined practice of Islam based on the Qur'an and the teaching of the prophet. They sought to purify Muslim belief and practice, and to abolish Sufi popular worship derived from Hindu and pagan customs. In the early nineteenth century there were Muslim reformist movements in the Northwest Frontier Provinces and Bengal, followed by an educational movement sponsored by the college at Deoband. The twentieth century has seen the rise of the Jami'at-i Ulama-i Hind, the Tablighi movement, and the Jama'at-i Islami of Mawdudi. Many of the religious leaders were hostile to the idea of an independent Muslim state and the secularism of the League's leading politicians and intellectuals, fearing that a new state would be secular in actuality though Muslim in name, unaccountable to the ulama and to the principles of Islam, and all the more dangerous because of its appeal to the communal sentiments of the populace. They believed it in the best interests of Muslims to preserve the unity of the Indian Muslim population inside a single Indian national state.

The struggle over a Muslim state, then, can be explained in terms of the legacy of a Mughal empire which had little formative effect upon the social and religious structures of the subcontinent, and allowed—even within the Muslim population—for a plurality of tribal, caste, occupational, ethnic, and political alternatives to Muslim and Mughal identity. Also the ambiguous Muslim credentials of the Mughal regime permitted Muslim religious movements to maintain their autonomy and to differentiate Muslim identity from political loyalty. Finally, the impact of European imperialism confirmed this pluralism, and locked the numerous fragments of the Indian population, Muslim and Hindu, into bitter struggle. The political elites sought to define an essentially secular position in terms of Muslim political symbols—the only symbols capable of rallying a fragmented Muslim society confronted with Hindu opposition—while the religious elites concentrated upon a moral and communal reform and were prepared to accept the establishment of a unified Indian national state.

This multi-sided struggle was won by the Muslim League with the support of shrine-oriented Sufis of the Punjab and United Provinces—not the ulama. Pakistan was created in 1947 as a Muslim state, the product of a history different from both that of Turkey and Iran by virtue of its Mughal heritage. Unlike the Ottoman empire and Turkey, the state lacked power; unlike Iran, the religious elites lacked unity; unlike both Turkey and Iran, the ethnic minorities had too much power. In Pakistan no coherent national identity has emerged. The state continues as in 1947 to appeal to Islam to overcome the pluralistic heritage of the subcontinent.

In sum, in the several states of the Middle East and South Asia, the historical variations in the relations of state, religious, and local elites and institutions help to explain the different roles and differing impacts of Islamic movements in these societies. In Turkey the dominant state institutions and the contemporary evolution of an economically and ideologically pluralistic society have limited Islamic religious revival to only a minority movement. In Egypt, by contrast, the political weakness and cultural ambivalence of successive governing elites, along with the lack of contemporary economic development, has allowed Islamic opposition movements to flourish. In Iran there is an historical confrontation between a weak state and relatively cohesive Islamic religious establishment, while in Pakistan, Islamic beliefs deprived of substantial institutional support are manipulated by an insecure political regime. Analysis of other Muslim world areas would, I think, further illustrate the importance of the structure of historic institutions for the expression and impact of Islamic revival movements.

V

CONCLUSION AND POLICY IMPLICATIONS

The Islamic revival can be viewed in two ways. From one perspective, it is a worldwide movement grounded in shared assumptions
about the relationship of individual religious morality and collective
political organization. From the other perspective, it is several movements, each manifesting itself within a regional and political context
and its religious and political prospects conditioned by particular
situations. From both these points of view, the Islamic revival is not
a temporary phenomenon or the result of foreign intervention and
manipulation. It rises out of political and cultural structures of Muslim societies going back to the eighteenth century and earlier, and
can only be understood as the expression of a deeply rooted and
persisting cultural mentality, and as part of the political processes in
Muslim countries.

The persistence of an historic cultural vocabulary is the essential
generating force behind successive Islamic revival movements. Islamic
religious values define an integral relationship between personal piety,
social solidarity, and political order. Movements based upon these
values arose first in the eighteenth century to correct the perceived
imbalances in traditional societies, then proved adaptable to differing
internal political situations, responsive to changes in international
power, and even to changes in class and social structure and in economic and technical conditions in modern societies. The cultural
vocabulary which they share is protean in its availability to social and
political causes. This vocabulary does not readily yield to modern
liberal, socialist, communist, or other ideologies, and is likely to
remain the basic language of moral and political conflict in Muslim
countries.

Islamic vocabulary persists and is not displaced by new secular ideologies for a number of reasons. While it has no appeal as ideology in western countries, its impact in its own sphere of cultural dominance cannot be overstated. Islamic vocabulary legitimates political and economic demands by presenting them in the guise of a higher ideal and by attaching them to personal piety and religious practice. Islamic commitments legitimate religious leadership and authority in political matters, and mobilize the support of displaced elements of the population (such as declining middle classes and aspiring student and professional elites) because Islamic symbols combine personal moral standards and communal solidarity and action with the struggle for political power. Islamic symbols also fuse a utopian hope—the hope of religious salvation cast in worldly terms—to concrete moral and political appeals. This condensation of several levels of psychological, social, and political concerns in the same symbols makes Islam a powerful motivating ideology.

Because of the universality, adaptability, and power of Islamic symbols, it is difficult to define the relationship they have to particular social groups or classes of people. Before the modern era, Islamic values served to legitimate political regimes, to define religious bodies such as schools of law and Sufi brotherhoods, and to articulate the political interests of small and parochial groups such as families, tribes, guilds, and fraternities. In the contemporary era, neo-Islamic rhetoric has been adopted by such diverse groups as small bazaar merchants, artisans, and workers in Indonesia, Iran, Egypt, and Turkey; by landless peasants in Malaysia and Nigeria; industrial workers in Algeria, Egypt, and Iran; and students and professional cadres in Turkey, Egypt, and Tunisia. While the inherent logic of the appeal of Islamic vocabulary to specific groups continues to elude us, clearly it has a profound appeal to both threatened and aspiring classes, who use it to articulate the need for political protection, on the one hand, and a restoration of the moral order, on the other. Islamic reform movements may be used for establishment purposes, but contemporary Islamic activism generally represents a minority opposition to the religious mentality, political power, and economic interests of the dominant groups in society and especially of the state elites.

Islamic revival movements are a sign of a struggle for power, and thus it is essential to understand the political contexts in which they operate to assess their appeal and their prospects for political success.

The conditions which determine the ability of Islamic movements to gain political dominance vary from country to country. The heritage of a strong state tradition and the subordination of Islamic religious elites to state bureaucracy has given enormous advantages to nationalist and secular influences in the former regions of the Ottoman empire—in Turkey, the Arab fertile crescent countries, Egypt, and parts of North Africa. While these countries have Islamic movements, military elites and secular ideologies remain in control. By contrast, the weakness of central states and the pluralism of organized religious life in the Indian subcontinent means that in Pakistan both state elites and religious opposition movements must appeal to Islamic values. Thus in any given context the potential power of an Islamic movement is constrained by the basic political structures of the society and, of course, by the opposition they engender.

Finally, Islamic movements have to be understood not only in terms of their cultural, sociological, and political origins, but also as the expression of a utopian dream which shatters all categories of analysis. Whatever their continuity with the historic past, the modern Islamic movements represent a profound transformation of the meaning of religious belief. Historically, religious belief was expressed through personal piety and communal identity, but the new movements turn religious feeling into social and political action. Traditionally, Islamic religious attitudes tended to be conservative, and to sanction and make sacred the world as it is; the new Islamic attitude wants to transform the world utterly in the name of the ideal. While traditional religious beliefs were grounded in the hope of salvation in the world to come, the revival forms of political Islam demand fulfillment in the here and now. They are a powerful psychological and political force precisely because they mobilize the religious yearning for salvation and project it into modern politics. The revival embodies a totalistic and utopian dream of a perfected human condition—not only in private morals but in political life, not in the next world but in this one.

Such profound cultural and political forces are bound to be a source of continuing tension within Muslim countries and in international affairs. Nevertheless no simple policy conclusions can be drawn about the role which the United States should attempt to play. If we understand Islamic movements in their cultural and political context, and observe them with some dispassion as a phenomenon intrinsic to a particular group of societies, we can see that our foreign policy faces basic dilemmas and must make basic compromises. On the one hand, failure to support friendly regimes leaves them militarily weakened, politically isolated, and in danger of subversion. On the other hand, even the strongest military and economic support has limited value. It will not win the full support of Muslim countries for our foreign policy goals. Over certain economic issues or certain political questions, such as Israel, there are real conflicts of interest. In any case, the governments of Muslim countries will not want to be or appear to be our puppets. Even though we think our embrace benign, they fear it. Many of them will be reluctant to allow the establishment of American military bases on their territory or even to give us consistent diplomatic support against the Soviet Union. Indeed, they may wish to maintain good relations with the Soviet Union to protect themselves against American pressures. Furthermore, they are aware that strong American support may have the paradoxical effect of weakening established regimes by compromising their legitimacy in the eyes of their Muslim opponents. American support for the shah of Iran was itself a major reason for the intensity of the opposition to him. While the close ties of the United States to Pakistan and Saudi Arabia are a source of military strength and of political stability in international relations, they compromise the domestic appeal of these regimes despite their Islamic credentials. If we wish to intervene in Muslim countries to protect sympathetic governments against their domestic opponents, our support must be tempered by the realization that states which are undergoing intense economic changes and social stresses are inherently vulnerable, and that regimes which have failed to achieve significant and fairly distributed economic gains, have suffered international political defeats, or are repressive of domestic opposition or corrupt in domestic administration are all the more vulnerable to internal resistance articulated in religious terms. Any policy toward Muslim countries will have to tread a delicate line, sensitive to changing currents of public opinion, between effective support and compromising association.

American and western attitudes toward Islamic religious and reform movements must be similarly nuanced. We may be antagonized by their fervor and strangeness, but experience shows that the behavior of states and powerful political movements is strongly affected by tactical considerations. They may contravene our values, but they cannot be taken as intrinsically hostile to our interests. No prior judgment can be made about whether such movements are favorable or unfavorable to us. Furthermore, it is crucial in dealing with such movements to distinguish between opposing political objectives which are threatening to American interests and hostility to Islam as such. Any suggestion that American or European (and therefore Christian) powers are hostile to Islam as a religion will only consolidate support for Islamic movements.

In any case, the issue is not to define a policy, for none can be defined to cope with so many and varied situations, but to build up a background of understanding which will help us understand their rhetorical position, their cultural strength, their active organization, and their place in the political system of their own societies, and to develop a mental posture of anticipation and readiness to cope with specific international complications as they arise. The demand upon us from a policy point of view is not to design a course of action but to cultivate an attitude of patient realism in dealing with a group of countries which are in the course of profound internal conflict over basic values, institutions, and the distribution of power. The policy questions which arise from the Islamic revival are not questions of manipulating or controlling a particular situation or of managing a crisis. They are questions about how to live with a long-term situation which has the potential of being vitally important in the political life of many third world countries—and our own—in unexpected ways.

IRA M. LAPIDUS is Professor of History at the University of California, Berkeley, where he also serves as chairman of the Center for Middle East Studies. His books include *Muslim Cities in the Later Middle Ages* (Harvard, 1967) and *Concise Cambridge History of Islamic Societies,* soon to be published by Cambridge University Press. He is also the editor of *Middle Eastern Cities: A Symposium on Ancient, Islamic, and Contemporary Middle Eastern Urbanism* (Berkeley, 1969).

INSTITUTE OF INTERNATIONAL STUDIES
UNIVERSITY OF CALIFORNIA, BERKELEY

215 Moses Hall   Berkeley, California 94720

CARL G. ROSBERG, *Director*

Monographs published by the Institute include:

RESEARCH SERIES

1. *The Chinese Anarchist Movement.* R.A. Scalapino and G.T. Yu. ($1.00)
7. *Birth Rates in Latin America.* O. Andrew Collver. ($2.50)
15. *Central American Economic Integration.* Stuart I. Fagan. ($2.00)
16. *The International Imperatives of Technology.* Eugene B. Skolnikoff. ($2.95)
17. *Autonomy or Dependence in Regional Integration.* P.C. Schmitter. ($1.75)
19. *Entry of New Competitors in Yugoslav Market Socialism.* S.R. Sacks. ($2.50)
20. *Political Integration in French-Speaking Africa.* Abdul A. Jalloh. ($3.50)
21. *The Desert & the Sown: Nomads in Wider Society.* Ed. C. Nelson. ($5.50)
22. *U.S.-Japanese Competition in International Markets.* J.E. Roemer. ($3.95)
23. *Political Disaffection Among British University Students.* J. Citrin and D.J.
    Elkins. ($2.00)
24. *Urban Inequality and Housing Policy in Tanzania.* Richard E. Stren. ($2.95)
25. *The Obsolescence of Regional Integration Theory.* Ernst B. Haas. ($4.95)
26. *The Voluntary Service Agency in Israel.* Ralph M. Kramer. ($2.00)
27. *The SOCSIM Microsimulation Program.* E. A. Hammel et al. ($4.50)
28. *Authoritarian Politics in Communist Europe.* Ed. Andrew C. Janos. ($3.95)
29. *The Anglo-Icelandic Cod War of 1972-1973.* Jeffrey A. Hart. ($2.00)
30. *Plural Societies and New States.* Robert Jackson. ($2.00)
31. *Politics of Oil Pricing in the Middle East, 1970-75.* R.C. Weisberg. ($4.95)
32. *Agricultural Policy and Performance in Zambia.* Doris J. Dodge. ($4.95)
33. *Five Classy Computer Programs.* E.A. Hammel & R.Z. Deuel. ($3.75)
34. *Housing the Urban Poor in Africa.* Richard E. Stren. ($5.95)
35. *The Russian New Right: Right-Wing Ideologies in USSR.* A. Yanov. ($5.95)
36. *Social Change in Romania, 1860-1940.* Ed. Kenneth Jowitt. ($4.50)
37. *The Leninist Response to National Dependency.* Kenneth Jowitt. ($4.95)
38. *Socialism in Sub-Saharan Africa.* Eds. C. Rosberg & T. Callaghy. ($12.95)
39. *Tanzania's Ujamaa Villages: Rural Development Strategy.* D. McHenry. ($5.95)
40. *Who Gains from Deep Ocean Mining?* I.G. Bulkley. ($3.50)
41. *Industrialization & the Nation-State in Peru.* Frits Wils. ($5.95)
42. *Ideology, Public Opinion, & Welfare Policy: Taxes and Spending in Indus-
    dustrialized Societies.* R.M. Coughlin. ($6.50)
43. *The Apartheid Regime: Political Power and Racial Domination.* Eds. R.M.
    Price and C. G. Rosberg. ($12.50)
44. *Yugoslav Economic System in the 1970s.* L.D. Tyson. ($5.50)
45. *Conflict in Chad.* Virginia Thompson & Richard Adloff. ($7.50)
46. *Conflict and Coexistence in Belgium.* Ed. Arend Lijphart. ($7.50)

47. *Changing Realities in Southern Africa.* Ed. Michael Clough. ($12.50)
48. *Nigerian Women Mobilized: Women's Political Activity in Southern Nigeria, 1900-1965.* Nina Emma Mba. ($12.95)
49. *Institutions of Rural Development for the Poor.* Ed. D. Leonard & D. Marshall. ($11.50)
50. *Politics of Women & Work in USSR & U.S.* J.C. Moses. ($9.50)
51. *Zionism and Territory.* Baruch Kimmerling. ($12.50)
52. *Soviet Subsidization of Trade with Eastern Europe.* M. Marrese & J. Vanous. ($14.50)
53. *Voluntary Efforts in Decentralized Management.* L. Ralston et al. ($9.00)

POLITICS OF MODERNIZATION SERIES

1. *Spanish Bureaucratic-Patrimonialism in America.* M. Sarfatti. ($2.00)
2. *Civil-Military Relations in Argentina, Chile, & Peru.* L. North. ($2.00)
9. *Modernization & Bureaucratic-Authoritarianism: Studies in South American Politics.* Guillermo O'Donnell. ($8.95)

POLICY PAPERS IN INTERNATIONAL AFFAIRS

1. *Images of Detente & the Soviet Political Order.* K. Jowitt. ($1.25)
2. *Detente After Brezhnev: Domestic Roots of Soviet Policy.* A. Yanov. ($4.50)
3. *Mature Neighbor Policy: A New Policy for Latin America.* A. Fishlow. ($3.95)
4. *Five Images of Soviet Future: Review & Synthesis.* G.W. Breslauer. ($4.50)
5. *Global Evangelism Rides Again: How to Protect Human Rights Without Really Trying.* E.B. Haas. ($2.95)
6. *Israel & Jordan: An Adversarial Partnership.* Ian Lustick. ($2.00)
7. *Political Syncretism in Italy.* Giuseppe Di Palma. ($3.95)
8. *U.S. Foreign Policy in Sub-Saharan Africa.* R.M. Price. ($4.50)
9. *East-West Technology Transfer in Perspective.* R.J. Carrick. ($5.50)
10. *NATO's Unremarked Demise.* Earl C. Ravenal. ($3.50)
11. *Toward Africanized Policy for Southern Africa.* R. Libby. ($5.50)
12. *Taiwan Relations Act & Defense of ROC.* E. Snyder et al. ($7.50)
13. *Cuba's Policy in Africa, 1959-1980.* William M. LeoGrande. ($4.50)
14. *Norway, NATO, & Forgotten Soviet Challenge.* K. Amundsen. ($2.95)
15. *Japanese Industrial Policy.* Ira Magaziner and Thomas Hout. ($6.50)
16. *Containment, Soviet Behavior, & Grand Strategy.* Robert Osgood. ($5.50)
17. *U.S.-Japanese Competition in Semiconductor Industry.* M. Borrus et al. ($7.50)